LOCAL SOURCING
AS A STRENGTH IN
NIGERIA'S SUPPLY CHAINS

MONSURAT ADEOLA ADEOSUN

Copyright © 2024. All Rights Reserved.

Local Sourcing as a Strength in Nigeria's Supply Chains
Monsurat Adeola Adeosun

No part of this publication may be reproduced, distributed, or transmitted in any form or by any means, including photocopying, recording, or other electronic or mechanical methods, without prior written permission from the copyright owner.

This material is provided solely for educational and informational purposes and should not be considered financial advice.

The author and publisher do not endorse any commercial products or services linked to this book.

Published in Nigeria, 2024 – Distributed Globally.

ISBN: 978-9-0752-7764-7

**Avid Books Publishing & Distribution Agency,
Lagos, Nigeria**

A catalogue record for this book is available at the National Library of Nigeria.

TABLE OF CONTENTS

TABLE OF CONTENTS .... **III**

PREFACE .... **V**

INTRODUCTION .... **VIII**

1. UNDERSTANDING SUPPLY CHAINS IN NIGERIA: AN OVERVIEW 1

2. THE CASE FOR LOCAL SOURCING: BENEFITS AND CHALLENGES 9

3. ECONOMIC IMPACT OF LOCAL SOURCING ON NIGERIAN INDUSTRIES 19

4. SUPPLY CHAIN RESILIENCE: LESSONS FROM GLOBAL DISRUPTIONS 29

5. AGRICULTURE AND LOCAL SOURCING: OPPORTUNITIES IN THE SECTOR 37

6. MANUFACTURING AND LOCAL SOURCING: BUILDING CAPACITY IN NIGERIA 45

7. TECHNOLOGY AND INNOVATION: ENABLING LOCAL SOURCING THROUGH DIGITALIZATION 51

8. INFRASTRUCTURAL BOTTLENECKS: CHALLENGES TO SCALING LOCAL SUPPLY CHAINS 59

9. GOVERNMENT POLICIES AND LOCAL SOURCING: ANALYZING THE ROLE OF POLICY FRAMEWORKS 67

10. CASE STUDIES: SUCCESSFUL LOCAL SOURCING IN NIGERIAN BUSINESSES 77

11. SUSTAINABILITY AND LOCAL SOURCING: THE ENVIRONMENTAL BENEFITS 85

12. FINANCING LOCAL SUPPLY CHAINS: ACCESS TO CREDIT AND INVESTMENT 93

13. PUBLIC-PRIVATE PARTNERSHIPS: COLLABORATING FOR SUPPLY CHAIN SUCCESS...101

14. TRAINING AND WORKFORCE DEVELOPMENT: EQUIPPING NIGERIANS FOR SUPPLY CHAIN MANAGEMENT 107

15. THE FUTURE OF LOCAL SOURCING IN NIGERIA: TRENDS AND PROJECTIONS 115

PREFACE

In a world where globalization dominates trade and commerce, local sourcing has often been overlooked in favor of cheaper, mass-produced goods from foreign markets. Yet, as we have seen through various global disruptions, the fragility of international supply chains can have devastating effects on both large economies and smaller ones alike. Nigeria, a nation with immense potential, rich natural resources, and a burgeoning population of over 200 million, stands at a critical junction. By embracing local sourcing, Nigeria has the opportunity to enhance its supply chains, create more jobs, boost its economy, and reduce its dependency on foreign imports. Local sourcing is not only an economic imperative but a necessary shift toward a more sustainable and resilient future for Nigeria.

The purpose of this book is to delve into how local sourcing can be a strategic strength within Nigeria's supply chains. We will explore the economic, social, and environmental benefits that can arise from greater reliance on local suppliers and producers. Moreover, we will discuss the challenges that local sourcing presents, such as infrastructural limitations, lack of skilled labor, and inconsistent policy frameworks. Through this analysis, we aim to provide practical solutions and strategies that can help stakeholders—including businesses, government agencies, and communities—maximize the potential of local sourcing in Nigeria.

Throughout the course of this book, we will examine real-world case studies, highlighting successful examples of Nigerian businesses and industries that have embraced local sourcing. From agricultural initiatives that support smallholder farmers to manufacturing processes that rely on homegrown materials, these examples will provide tangible insights into how local sourcing can be implemented effectively. We will also examine the role that government policy and public-private partnerships can play in fostering an environment conducive to local sourcing. By doing so, we hope to demonstrate that local sourcing is not just a theoretical concept but a pragmatic and impactful approach that can transform Nigeria's economic landscape.

This book is intended for a wide range of readers, including students, researchers, policymakers, business leaders, and supply chain professionals. Our goal is to inspire a shift in thinking about supply chain management, moving away from the traditional focus on globalization and efficiency toward a more balanced approach that values resilience, sustainability, and local empowerment.

We extend our deepest gratitude to the many individuals and organizations who contributed their insights and expertise to this book. Their experience has been invaluable in shaping the ideas presented here. It is our hope that this book will serve as a valuable resource for all those interested in the future of supply chain management in Nigeria and beyond.

INTRODUCTION

In today's globalized world, supply chains have become more complex and interconnected than ever before. Goods and services now traverse vast distances, crossing multiple borders before they reach their final destinations. This global web of suppliers, manufacturers, and retailers has, in many ways, made goods more affordable and accessible to consumers worldwide. However, as recent global events have shown, such as the COVID-19 pandemic and various geopolitical conflicts, the very interconnectedness that makes global supply chains efficient also makes them vulnerable. When one link in the chain is disrupted, the effects can ripple across industries and economies, causing widespread shortages, delays, and financial losses.

In Nigeria, the consequences of global supply chain disruptions are particularly acute. As one of the largest economies in Africa, Nigeria is heavily dependent on imports for a wide range of products, from raw materials to finished goods. This reliance on foreign suppliers leaves the country vulnerable to external shocks, whether they be price fluctuations in global markets, logistical bottlenecks, or trade restrictions. In recent years, Nigeria has experienced several such shocks, which have highlighted the need for a more resilient and self-reliant approach to supply chain management. This is where local sourcing comes into play.

Local sourcing refers to the practice of procuring goods and services from suppliers that are based within a country or region, as opposed to relying on international suppliers. In the context of Nigeria, local sourcing offers several potential benefits. It can reduce the country's dependency on foreign imports, shorten lead times, lower transportation costs, and stimulate domestic industries. Moreover, local sourcing can create jobs, support small and medium-sized enterprises (SMEs), and contribute to a more equitable distribution of wealth within the country. From an environmental perspective, local sourcing can also help reduce the carbon footprint associated with long-distance transportation and promote more sustainable production practices.

This book will explore the many facets of local sourcing in Nigeria's supply chains. We will begin by providing an overview of Nigeria's current supply chain landscape, highlighting the key sectors involved and the challenges they face. From there, we will delve into the benefits of local sourcing, examining how it can improve supply chain resilience, boost economic development, and foster sustainability. We will also discuss the obstacles that need to be overcome to make local sourcing a viable and widespread practice in Nigeria, such as inadequate infrastructure, limited access to financing, and regulatory hurdles.

In addition to theoretical analysis, this book will feature practical insights from real-world case studies. We will look at successful examples of local sourcing in industries such as agriculture, manufacturing, and technology, showcasing how Nigerian businesses have integrated local suppliers into their supply chains. These case studies will provide valuable lessons for other businesses and policymakers seeking to adopt local sourcing as part of their supply chain strategy.

The role of government policy will also be a key focus of this book. Local sourcing cannot thrive without the right regulatory environment, and we will examine the policy frameworks that are needed to support local suppliers and foster collaboration between the public and private sectors. In doing so, we will highlight the importance of public-private partnerships in driving innovation, investment, and workforce development.

Ultimately, this book aims to provide a comprehensive understanding of local sourcing as a strategic tool for strengthening Nigeria's supply chains. Whether you are a business leader looking to improve your supply chain operations, a policymaker seeking to promote economic growth, or a researcher interested in the future of supply chain management, we hope that this book will offer valuable insights and practical recommendations. By the end of this journey, we hope to have convinced you that local sourcing is not just a possibility for Nigeria, it is an imperative for building a more resilient, prosperous, and sustainable future.

CHAPTER 1

UNDERSTANDING SUPPLY CHAINS IN NIGERIA: AN OVERVIEW

Supply chains form the backbone of any economy, and Nigeria's supply chains are no different. They serve as the lifeline for the movement of goods, services, raw materials, and finished products across the nation and to international markets. These supply chains connect farmers, manufacturers, service providers, distributors, retailers, and consumers in intricate networks. However, Nigeria's supply chains are far more complex due to several factors such as geographical diversity, economic disparity, inadequate infrastructure, policy inconsistencies, and socio-political instability. All of these factors add layers of complexity that create significant inefficiencies in how goods and services move within the country.

A supply chain can be understood as the complete flow of processes involved in producing and distributing a product—from raw material extraction, manufacturing, and assembly to distribution and final delivery to the consumer. It includes the activities of sourcing, production, logistics, warehousing, and even after-sales services. Each link in the chain is crucial to maintaining the efficiency of the entire system. In Nigeria, supply chains span across critical sectors such as agriculture, manufacturing, oil and gas, retail, and services, but they are often hampered by structural challenges unique to the Nigerian context.

The agricultural sector is particularly notable in the Nigerian supply chain landscape due to its sheer size and importance. Agriculture employs around 70% of Nigeria's workforce and contributes significantly to the country's GDP. However, despite its significance, the agricultural supply chain faces numerous hurdles. For example, poor road networks, unreliable electricity, and a lack of adequate cold storage infrastructure contribute to high post-harvest losses. Smallholder farmers, who form the bulk of Nigeria's agricultural producers, often struggle to bring their products to market in time or to retain their crops' quality. Additionally, the underdeveloped logistics sector makes it difficult for these farmers to access urban markets or engage in export opportunities, limiting their potential income and reducing the overall efficiency of the supply chain.

Beyond agriculture, Nigeria's manufacturing sector plays an equally critical role in the economy. However, it faces its own unique set of challenges. Many Nigerian manufacturers are heavily reliant on imported raw materials, which exposes them to fluctuations in international commodity prices and currency volatility. For instance, a Nigerian company manufacturing plastics may import the majority of its resin from overseas markets. This reliance increases production costs and makes the final product less competitive in both local and international markets. Compounding this issue is the country's inconsistent power supply. The high cost of running diesel generators adds to operational expenses, eroding profit margins and making local products less price-competitive compared to imports.

Even though the services sector, particularly logistics and transportation, plays a pivotal role in the efficient functioning of supply chains, it is plagued by inefficiencies. The transport sector, including road, rail, and sea freight, is notoriously unreliable in Nigeria. Congested ports, poorly maintained roads, insufficient rail networks, and bureaucratic bottlenecks at customs checkpoints cause delays in the movement of goods, resulting in higher operational costs for businesses. For example, Lagos, Nigeria's economic hub, suffers from severe port congestion, leading to long waiting times for ships and delays in clearing goods. This inefficiency not only impacts logistics companies but also ripples across the broader economy, affecting industries that depend on the timely delivery of raw materials and finished goods.

In addition to infrastructure, the regulatory framework governing supply chains in Nigeria presents significant challenges. The regulatory environment can be unpredictable, with frequent changes in trade policies, tariffs, and import restrictions. This creates an atmosphere of uncertainty for businesses that need to make long-term strategic decisions. For example, changes in tariffs on certain imported goods can disrupt supply chains, as businesses are forced to adjust their sourcing strategies to remain profitable. Moreover, corruption and bureaucratic inefficiencies in regulatory bodies, including the Nigerian Customs Service, further complicate matters, resulting in delays and increased costs for businesses trying to navigate the regulatory landscape.

Furthermore, workforce capacity plays a crucial role in the efficiency of supply chains. Nigeria's growing population presents a massive labor force, but there are significant gaps in the technical and operational skills required to support modern supply chain management practices. Many workers in Nigeria, especially in rural and semi-urban areas, lack formal training in logistics, manufacturing, and quality control. This skills gap makes it difficult for Nigerian businesses to optimize their supply chains or implement advanced technologies like automation, data analytics, or artificial intelligence that are increasingly becoming standard in global supply chain management.

These challenges notwithstanding, Nigeria's supply chains also present immense opportunities. The country's vast natural resources, including agricultural products, minerals, and oil, offer significant potential for growth in local production and sourcing. Additionally, Nigeria's strategic location as a gateway to West Africa positions it as a potential logistics and manufacturing hub for the entire region. If the challenges in infrastructure, workforce development, and regulatory frameworks can be addressed, Nigeria's supply chains could become a powerful driver of economic growth, attracting investment and fostering sustainable development.

The Nigerian government has recently shown a greater commitment to addressing these infrastructural and regulatory challenges. Large-scale infrastructure projects are underway, such as expanding and upgrading the country's road and rail networks, modernizing the seaports, and improving energy distribution. Additionally, policy reforms aimed at reducing bureaucratic red tape and creating more business-friendly environments are being implemented. For instance, customs procedures are being streamlined to reduce delays at ports, and there is an increasing push to digitize regulatory processes to improve transparency and efficiency.

Moreover, there is growing interest in incorporating technology into Nigeria's supply chains. The rise of e-commerce platforms, digital procurement solutions, and logistics tracking systems offers a glimpse into the future of Nigerian supply chains, where digitalization can significantly reduce inefficiencies and improve the flow of goods and services. Nigerian businesses, both large and small, are beginning to recognize the potential of technology to transform their supply chain operations, and the adoption of digital tools is steadily increasing.

Despite these positive developments, there is still a long way to go before Nigeria's supply chains can reach their full potential. Addressing the deep-rooted challenges in infrastructure, regulation, and workforce capacity will require sustained effort, investment, and collaboration between the public and private sectors. However, the potential rewards are immense: a more efficient, resilient, and competitive supply chain system could transform

Nigeria's economy, fostering industrialization, reducing unemployment, and improving living standards across the country.

The role of the private sector will be crucial in this transformation. Private businesses must take the initiative to invest in their supply chains, whether by upgrading their infrastructure, adopting new technologies, or improving their workforce through training and capacity building. Partnerships between the private sector and the government can also help drive progress, with the government providing the necessary regulatory framework and infrastructure investments, while private businesses contribute their expertise and resources to improve supply chain efficiency.

Additionally, international investors and development partners can play a significant role in supporting the development of Nigeria's supply chains. By investing in infrastructure projects, technology solutions, and capacity-building programs, international organizations can help accelerate the pace of reform and ensure that Nigeria's supply chains become more competitive and resilient.

In conclusion, Nigeria's supply chains are at a critical juncture. While they are currently hampered by significant challenges, they also offer tremendous opportunities for growth and development. By addressing the structural issues in infrastructure, regulation, and workforce capacity, Nigeria can unlock the full potential of its supply chains and position itself as a major player in the global economy. The journey will not be easy, but with the right investments and policies, Nigeria's supply chains can become a powerful engine for economic growth, job creation, and sustainable development.

CHAPTER 2

THE CASE FOR LOCAL SOURCING: BENEFITS AND CHALLENGES

Local sourcing has become a vital topic in supply chain management across the globe, particularly in light of recent disruptions caused by geopolitical conflicts, global pandemics, and shifting trade dynamics. Businesses and governments alike are recognizing the importance of building resilient and sustainable supply chains that can withstand external shocks. For Nigeria, local sourcing offers a significant opportunity to reduce dependency on imports, stimulate local industries, create jobs, and foster economic development.

One of the primary benefits of local sourcing is cost reduction. By sourcing goods and services from local suppliers, businesses can significantly reduce transportation costs, which are often one of the largest expenses in supply chains. In Nigeria, where transportation infrastructure is underdeveloped and fuel costs are high, cutting down on the distance goods need to travel can lead to considerable savings. Shorter supply chains also mean shorter lead times, which can be a game-changer in sectors such as retail and manufacturing, where speed to market is crucial. Local suppliers can typically deliver goods faster than international suppliers, reducing the risk of stock-outs and enabling businesses to respond more quickly to changes in demand.

Another key benefit of local sourcing is job creation. Small and medium-sized enterprises (SMEs), which form the backbone of Nigeria's economy, often struggle to compete with larger, international corporations that can offer lower prices due to economies of scale. By prioritizing local sourcing, businesses can provide opportunities for SMEs to participate in formal supply chains, giving them access to larger markets and helping them grow. This, in turn, leads to job creation, as local suppliers expand their operations to meet the increased demand. The ripple effect of job creation extends beyond the direct beneficiaries of local sourcing, families, communities, and entire regions benefit when local businesses thrive.

Furthermore, local sourcing also promotes economic self-sufficiency. Nigeria's reliance on imports has long made its economy vulnerable to external shocks, such as global commodity price fluctuations and supply chain disruptions.

By sourcing goods locally, Nigeria can reduce its dependency on imports, making its economy more resilient to these external shocks. For example, if global shipping routes are disrupted, businesses that rely heavily on imports may experience delays and increased costs. However, businesses that source locally can continue to operate with minimal disruption, as they are less reliant on international supply chains. This increased resilience is especially important in critical industries such as healthcare, agriculture, and energy, where disruptions in supply can have significant social and economic consequences.

Local sourcing also has a significant environmental impact, as it reduces the carbon footprint associated with the transportation of goods over long distances. In the face of growing concerns over climate change, businesses are increasingly being held accountable for their environmental practices. By sourcing locally, businesses can reduce the emissions associated with shipping goods internationally, particularly when air and sea freight are involved. This is particularly important for Nigeria, where environmental degradation from pollution, deforestation, and resource extraction is already a pressing concern. By reducing the environmental impact of their supply chains, businesses can contribute to more sustainable production and consumption patterns.

However, the potential benefits of local sourcing in Nigeria must be weighed against several significant challenges. One of the most pressing challenges is the lack of infrastructure necessary to support efficient local supply chains. As discussed in Chapter 1, poor road networks, unreliable power supply, and insufficient storage and logistics facilities all make it difficult for local suppliers to meet the needs of businesses, particularly in industries where timely delivery and consistent quality are critical. For example, in the agricultural sector, a lack of cold storage facilities often leads to high levels of spoilage, reducing the quantity and quality of food that reaches consumers. For local sourcing to become a widespread and viable practice, significant investments in infrastructure will be necessary.

The availability and quality of raw materials also pose a challenge to local sourcing. While Nigeria is rich in natural resources, many industries still rely on imported materials due to issues related to the extraction, refinement, and processing of local resources. For example, the manufacturing sector often imports steel, chemicals, and plastics because locally sourced alternatives are either unavailable or of insufficient quality. Without improvements in local raw material production and processing capabilities, businesses may struggle to find local suppliers that can meet their needs at the required scale and quality.

Workforce capacity is another critical challenge. Many industries in Nigeria suffer from a shortage of skilled workers who have the technical expertise required to produce goods at the quality levels demanded by larger businesses. This skills gap is particularly evident in sectors such as manufacturing and construction, where advanced machinery and processes are becoming increasingly common. For local sourcing initiatives to succeed, businesses will need to invest in training programs that equip workers with the skills needed to meet the technical demands of modern industries. Additionally, partnerships between educational institutions and businesses can help ensure that the next generation of workers is prepared to support the growth of local industries.

Furthermore, innovation plays a key role in overcoming some of these challenges. Investing in research and development (R&D) can improve the efficiency and sustainability of local production processes. For example, developing new farming techniques or manufacturing technologies that are adapted to the local context could help businesses reduce costs and improve the quality of locally produced goods. By fostering a culture of innovation, Nigeria can improve its competitiveness on the global stage and ensure that its local industries remain viable in the long term.

Despite these challenges, local sourcing presents a wealth of opportunities for businesses willing to invest in their supply chains and adapt to the unique conditions of the Nigerian market. Government policies, such as incentives for local sourcing or investments in infrastructure, can play a critical role in supporting these efforts. For example, tax breaks or subsidies for businesses that source locally could encourage more companies to adopt local sourcing practices. Additionally, investments in infrastructure, such as roads, energy, and telecommunications, would improve the efficiency of local supply chains and make it easier for businesses to operate.

Additionally, government initiatives focused on import substitution can create a more conducive environment for local sourcing. Import substitution policies aim to reduce dependency on foreign goods by encouraging the production of local alternatives. This can be achieved through protective tariffs on imports, subsidies for local industries, or government procurement policies that prioritize locally produced goods and services. By creating a level playing field for local businesses, import substitution policies can help foster the development of domestic industries and reduce Nigeria's reliance on imports.

Public-private partnerships (PPPs) are another potential solution to the challenges of local sourcing. By collaborating with the private sector, the government can leverage additional resources and expertise to invest in infrastructure, workforce development, and innovation. For example, a PPP could involve the construction of a cold storage facility that serves local farmers, reducing post-harvest losses and improving the availability of fresh produce in urban markets. Similarly, partnerships between businesses and educational institutions can help develop training programs that equip workers with the skills needed to support local industries.

Moreover, addressing the regulatory barriers that hinder local sourcing will be essential for its success. Inconsistent policies, bureaucratic delays, and corruption can create significant obstacles for businesses looking to source locally. For example, changes in tariffs on imported goods can make it difficult for local suppliers to compete with international competitors, while cumbersome regulatory processes can slow down the delivery of goods and materials. Streamlining regulations, improving transparency, and creating a more business-friendly environment will be critical for encouraging local sourcing.

Another key challenge is the perception of quality associated with locally sourced goods. Some businesses and consumers may believe that locally produced goods are of lower quality than imported alternatives, which can limit the demand for locally sourced products. Overcoming this perception will require investments in quality control and assurance processes that ensure locally produced goods meet international standards. By improving the quality and reliability of locally sourced goods, businesses can build trust with consumers and create a stronger market for local products.

Local sourcing also presents opportunities for greater economic inclusion, particularly for marginalized communities. Many rural areas in Nigeria are home to small-scale producers who have traditionally been excluded from formal supply chains due to their geographic isolation or lack of market access. By creating more direct links between these producers and businesses, local sourcing can help bring these communities into a formal economy, providing them with greater economic opportunities and improving their livelihoods. This, in turn, can contribute to broader efforts to reduce poverty and promote inclusive economic development.

In conclusion, local sourcing offers a powerful tool for driving economic growth, job creation, and poverty reduction in Nigeria. By reducing reliance on imports, local sourcing can help Nigeria build a more resilient and self-sufficient economy. However, realizing the full potential of local sourcing will require addressing significant challenges, including infrastructure deficits, workforce capacity, regulatory barriers, and perceptions of quality. By investing in infrastructure, workforce development, innovation, and regulatory reform, Nigeria can unlock the full potential of local sourcing and build more resilient, sustainable, and inclusive supply chains. As businesses begin to recognize the benefits of sourcing locally, they can play a key role in supporting the development of local industries and contributing to the broader economic development of the country.

The case for local sourcing in Nigeria is compelling. With the right support from government, the private sector, and international development partners, local sourcing can become a cornerstone of Nigeria's economic strategy, helping the country transition from an import-dependent economy to one that is more self-reliant, resilient, and sustainable.

CHAPTER 3

ECONOMIC IMPACT OF LOCAL SOURCING ON NIGERIAN INDUSTRIES

The integration of local sourcing into Nigeria's industries has the potential to reshape the country's economic landscape dramatically. By relying on domestic resources and fostering local industries, businesses can reduce their dependency on volatile global markets, increase their production capacity, and drive sustainable economic growth. Local sourcing offers benefits not only to individual businesses but also to the broader Nigerian economy, contributing to job creation, poverty reduction, and the overall enhancement of economic resilience.

In the agricultural sector, which remains the backbone of Nigeria's economy, local sourcing can catalyze transformative change. Presently, a large number of smallholder farmers operate outside formal supply chains, selling their produce in informal markets where they often receive lower prices and face income instability. Local sourcing can help address these challenges by creating more direct and structured relationships between smallholder farmers and businesses. For instance, food processing companies or large retailers can form partnerships with local farmers to source raw materials such as cassava, cocoa, and palm oil directly from them, ensuring fair pricing and market access. This creates a sustainable business ecosystem where farmers receive consistent income, and businesses benefit from a steady supply of locally sourced materials, reducing reliance on imports.

Local sourcing in agriculture also opens up opportunities for value addition. Nigeria has historically been an exporter of raw agricultural products like cocoa beans, palm oil, and cashew nuts, often missing out on the significant value-added potential in processing these goods. By investing in agro-processing industries, Nigeria can capture a larger share of the value chain domestically. For example, rather than exporting raw cocoa beans, Nigeria could develop its own chocolate manufacturing industry, thereby creating jobs in manufacturing, packaging, marketing, and retail. Such investments not only boost the agricultural sector but also create downstream opportunities in other industries, driving economic diversification and making Nigeria less dependent on global commodity price fluctuations.

Furthermore, local sourcing in agriculture can improve food security by reducing Nigeria's reliance on imported food products. Currently, Nigeria imports large quantities of staple foods such as rice, wheat, and fish to meet domestic demand. This dependence on imported food leaves the country vulnerable to global supply chain disruptions, as seen during the COVID-19 pandemic, when many countries faced food shortages due to restrictions on international trade. By sourcing food locally and supporting domestic agricultural production, Nigeria can ensure a more stable and affordable food supply, while also reducing the outflow of foreign exchange used to purchase imported food.

The benefits of local sourcing extend beyond agriculture. In the manufacturing sector, local sourcing can stimulate industrial growth by lowering the costs associated with importing raw materials and components. Nigeria's manufacturing industry has traditionally been hampered by high production costs, in part because manufacturers rely heavily on imports for essential inputs such as steel, plastics, and chemicals. This reliance makes local manufacturers vulnerable to fluctuations in global commodity prices and currency exchange rates, which can increase production costs and reduce their competitiveness in both domestic and international markets.

By encouraging local sourcing, Nigeria can mitigate these risks and boost the resilience of its manufacturing sector. For instance, the Nigerian cement industry has already demonstrated the potential benefits of local sourcing by utilizing locally available limestone, which has helped reduce production costs and meet growing domestic demand for construction materials. This model can be applied to other industries such as textiles, automotive, and consumer goods, where locally sourced raw materials can replace imported alternatives, leading to more competitive pricing and a more sustainable manufacturing ecosystem.

Local sourcing also fosters innovation. As manufacturers increasingly turn to local suppliers, they drive the need for improved production processes, higher-quality materials, and new technologies. This creates opportunities for local businesses to invest in research and development (R&D), adopt advanced manufacturing techniques, and build sophisticated production capabilities. By fostering innovation within domestic supply chains, Nigerian industries can not only improve their efficiency and quality but also become more competitive in regional and global markets.

In the technology sector, local sourcing presents an exciting opportunity for economic growth and the development of homegrown solutions. Nigeria's technology industry is rapidly expanding, with companies in fintech, e-commerce, and mobile technology gaining international recognition. By sourcing locally, tech companies can strengthen Nigeria's domestic tech ecosystem and foster innovation tailored to the specific needs of Nigerian consumers and businesses. For example, tech companies could collaborate with local research institutions and universities to develop hardware and software solutions that are optimized for the Nigerian market, such as affordable smartphones, mobile payment systems, and agricultural technology tools. This approach not only reduces the reliance on imported technology but also positions Nigeria as a leader in digital innovation within Africa.

The economic impact of local sourcing extends beyond the benefits to individual industries; it also has significant macroeconomic implications for Nigeria's broader economy. One of the most immediate benefits of local sourcing is its potential to reduce the country's trade deficit. Nigeria currently imports a wide range of goods, from agricultural products to industrial machinery and consumer goods, which drains foreign exchange reserves and contributes to the country's persistent trade imbalance. By promoting local sourcing, Nigeria can reduce its reliance on imports, conserve foreign exchange, and improve its balance of payments. This can help stabilize the naira, reduce inflationary pressures, and create a more predictable economic environment for businesses and consumers.

Local sourcing also generates new business opportunities, creating a multiplier effect throughout the economy. As businesses increasingly source from local suppliers, demand for domestically produced goods and services rises. This demand can drive the expansion of existing businesses and encourage the creation of new enterprises, particularly in rural areas where formal employment opportunities are often limited. For example, a local manufacturer sourcing packaging materials from a nearby supplier may, in turn, create demand for local logistics providers, maintenance services, and raw material producers. The resulting job creation benefits not only the immediate supply chain but also the broader economy, as workers and businesses contribute to local economies by spending their incomes on goods and services.

Additionally, local sourcing enhances income generation for workers and businesses across the supply chain. When businesses invest in local suppliers, they are more likely to provide support in the form of training, equipment, and capacity-building initiatives. This investment helps local suppliers improve their productivity and profitability, which in turn leads to higher wages for workers and greater revenues for businesses. These gains contribute to broader economic development and poverty reduction, as more people gain access to stable, well-paying jobs and businesses experience increases profitability.

Tax revenues for the government also stand to benefit from the growth of local sourcing. As local businesses expand and generate higher incomes, they contribute more to the tax base through corporate taxes, value-added taxes (VAT), and other forms of taxation. These additional revenues can be used by the government to fund critical public services such as education, healthcare, and infrastructure development, all of which are essential for long-term economic growth and prosperity.

Moreover, local sourcing can foster economic resilience by reducing Nigeria's exposure to external shocks. The global economy is increasingly interconnected, and disruptions in international supply chains whether due to geopolitical conflicts, trade disputes, or pandemics can have significant repercussions for countries that rely heavily on imports. By developing robust local supply chains, Nigeria can insulate itself from these external shocks, ensuring that businesses can continue to operate even when global supply chains are disrupted. A more resilient economy is better equipped to withstand crises, recover more quickly, and maintain steady growth over the long term.

The benefits of local sourcing extend to the social and environmental realms as well. Local sourcing can contribute to greater social inclusion by creating opportunities for small-scale producers, women-owned businesses, and marginalized communities to participate in formal supply chains. In many cases, these groups have been excluded from traditional supply chains due to their geographic isolation, lack of access to credit, or other barriers. By promoting local sourcing, businesses can create more inclusive supply chains that benefit a wider range of stakeholders.

From an environmental perspective, local sourcing offers the potential to reduce the carbon footprint associated with long-distance transportation. By sourcing goods locally, businesses can reduce the need for air and sea freight, which are major contributors to greenhouse gas emissions. This reduction in transportation-related emissions is particularly important in the context of climate change, as businesses are increasingly being held accountable for their environmental impact. By adopting more sustainable sourcing practices, Nigerian businesses can contribute to global efforts to combat climate change while also improving their own operational efficiency.

In conclusion, local sourcing presents a transformative opportunity for Nigeria's economy. By promoting local production, businesses can reduce their reliance on imports, create jobs, drive innovation, and enhance the resilience of their supply chains. The ripple effects of local sourcing extend beyond individual businesses to the broader economy, contributing to poverty reduction, economic diversification, and sustainable growth. As more Nigerian businesses and policymakers embrace local sourcing, the country stands to gain not only in terms of immediate economic benefits but also in terms of long-term development and prosperity. Local sourcing is not just a business strategy; it is a pathway to a more self-sufficient, resilient, and inclusive Nigerian economy.

CHAPTER 4

SUPPLY CHAIN RESILIENCE: LESSONS FROM GLOBAL DISRUPTIONS

In recent years, the fragility of global supply chains has been laid bare by a series of disruptive events, most notably the COVID-19 pandemic. Factory shutdowns, shipping delays, and logistical bottlenecks brought global trade to a standstill, exposing the vulnerabilities of highly interconnected supply chains. For a country like Nigeria, where many industries rely on imports for essential goods and raw materials, these disruptions highlighted the urgent need for a more resilient supply chain strategy. Local sourcing has emerged as a key solution to this challenge, offering a way to reduce dependency on international suppliers and build stronger, more adaptable supply chains.

One of the most significant lessons from the COVID-19 pandemic is the importance of diversification in supply chains. Many businesses around the world were caught off guard when their primary suppliers were unable to deliver goods due to lockdowns, transportation restrictions, or other pandemic-related disruptions. In Nigeria, where industries such as healthcare and manufacturing depend heavily on imports, these disruptions led to shortages of critical goods, including medical equipment, pharmaceuticals, and raw materials for manufacturing. By promoting local sourcing, businesses can diversify their supply base and reduce their reliance on a small number of international suppliers, making their supply chains more resilient to future disruptions.

Local sourcing offers several key advantages in terms of resilience. First and foremost, it reduces lead times. When businesses source goods from international suppliers, they are often subject to long lead times, which can be further exacerbated by delays in shipping, customs clearance, or transportation. Local sourcing, by contrast, allows businesses to source goods and materials from suppliers that are geographically closer, resulting in shorter lead times and more agile supply chains. This increased agility enables businesses to respond more quickly to changes in demand, production issues, or external shocks, ensuring that they can continue to operate even in the face of disruptions.

In addition to reducing lead times, local sourcing also fosters stronger relationships between businesses and suppliers. These relationships are critical for supply chain resilience, as they create a foundation of trust, collaboration, and communication. In times of crisis, businesses that have established strong relationships with local suppliers are better positioned to secure critical supplies, negotiate favorable terms, and find innovative solutions to supply chain challenges. For example, a local manufacturer may be more willing to adjust production schedules, provide alternative materials, or offer flexible payment terms during a crisis, ensuring that both the supplier and the business can weather the storm.

Diversification of suppliers is another important aspect of local sourcing for resilience. Global supply chains often rely on a small number of suppliers for critical goods or materials, increasing the risk of supply chain disruptions if one supplier faces production issues or delays. Local sourcing, however, allows businesses to diversify their supplier base by working with multiple local suppliers. This diversification not only reduces the risk of supply chain disruptions but also creates healthy competition among suppliers, which can lead to better pricing, improved quality, and more innovative solutions.

The importance of local sourcing for supply chain resilience was further underscored during the pandemic, particularly in the healthcare sector. As global supply chains for medical equipment, pharmaceuticals, and personal protective equipment (PPE) were severely disrupted, Nigeria and many other countries faced critical shortages of essential healthcare supplies. Local manufacturers stepped in to fill the gap, producing masks, ventilators, and other medical supplies that were desperately needed by hospitals and healthcare workers. This shift toward local production not only helped alleviate immediate shortages but also demonstrated the capacity of Nigerian businesses to adapt and respond to supply chain disruptions.

In the food and agriculture sectors, local sourcing also played a crucial role in ensuring supply chain resilience during the pandemic. Global disruptions to food supply chains, including restrictions on international trade, labor shortages, and transportation bottlenecks, led to food shortages and price increases in many parts of the world. In Nigeria, where food security is already a pressing issue, these disruptions could have had catastrophic consequences. However, local farmers and food producers stepped up to mitigate the impact of global disruptions by increasing domestic food production and ensuring a steady supply of staple crops such as rice, maize, and cassava. This experience highlighted the importance of local sourcing in building a more self-sufficient and resilient food system.

Local sourcing also contributes to supply chain resilience by reducing the environmental risks associated with long-distance transportation. Global supply chains are highly dependent on international shipping and air freight, both of which are vulnerable to disruptions caused by natural disasters, extreme weather events, or political instability. Local sourcing, by contrast, relies on shorter transportation routes, which are less exposed to these risks. Additionally, by reducing the distance that goods need to travel, local sourcing can help businesses lower their carbon footprint, contributing to greater sustainability and environmental resilience.

Despite the clear benefits of local sourcing for supply chain resilience, several challenges must be addressed to fully realize its potential. One of the most significant challenges is the capacity of local suppliers to meet the needs of large businesses. In many cases, local suppliers in Nigeria lack the resources, technology, or expertise needed to produce goods at the scale or quality required by larger businesses. This capacity gap can make it difficult for businesses to rely on local suppliers for critical goods or materials, particularly in industries such as manufacturing or technology.

Another challenge is the need for investment in local infrastructure. Nigeria's transportation, energy, and communication infrastructure remain underdeveloped in many areas, which can hinder the ability of local suppliers to deliver goods efficiently and reliably. Without significant improvements in infrastructure, businesses may continue to face logistical challenges when sourcing locally, limiting the effectiveness of local sourcing as a resilience strategy.

Despite these challenges, the potential for local sourcing to enhance supply chain resilience in Nigeria is significant. By investing in local suppliers, improving infrastructure, and fostering collaboration between businesses and government, Nigeria can build more resilient supply chains that are better equipped to withstand future crises. Local sourcing offers a pathway to greater self-reliance, reduced exposure to global risks, and a more sustainable and inclusive economy.

The lessons learned from the COVID-19 pandemic and other global disruptions should inform Nigeria's approach to supply chain management. By prioritizing local sourcing, diversifying suppliers, and investing in infrastructure, Nigeria can build a more resilient economy that is better prepared to navigate future crises. Local sourcing is not just a short-term solution to the challenges of global disruptions; it is a long-term strategy for building stronger, more adaptable, and more sustainable supply chains.

In conclusion, the global disruptions of recent years have exposed the vulnerabilities of interconnected supply chains and highlighted the need for a more resilient approach. Local sourcing offers a powerful solution to these challenges, allowing businesses to reduce their reliance on international suppliers, shorten lead times, diversify their supply base, and build stronger relationships with local suppliers. By embracing local sourcing, Nigeria can build more resilient supply chains that are capable of withstanding future disruptions and driving sustainable economic growth.

CHAPTER 5

AGRICULTURE AND LOCAL SOURCING: OPPORTUNITIES IN THE SECTOR

Agriculture has long been the cornerstone of Nigeria's economy, employing around 70% of the workforce and contributing significantly to the country's GDP. The sector has vast potential for growth, thanks to Nigeria's rich natural resources, including arable land, favorable climatic conditions, and a large labor force. However, despite these advantages, agriculture in Nigeria remains underdeveloped, with inefficiencies, high post-harvest losses, and limited access to markets impeding the sector's ability to reach its full potential. Local sourcing offers a critical opportunity to address these challenges by creating more resilient, efficient, and inclusive agricultural supply chains. By investing in local farmers and sourcing food and raw materials domestically, businesses can help transform Nigeria's agricultural sector, improving productivity, reducing dependency on imports, and ensuring greater food security.

The Nigerian agricultural supply chain is dominated by smallholder farmers, who account for the majority of the country's agricultural output. These farmers often work on small plots of land using traditional farming methods, with limited access to modern technologies, inputs, and formal markets. As a result, they face significant challenges in bringing their products to market, particularly in urban centers where demand is highest. Poor infrastructure, including inadequate roads, a lack of cold storage, and unreliable electricity, further exacerbate these challenges, leading to high post-harvest losses and reduced incomes for farmers.

Local sourcing offers a powerful solution to many of these challenges by creating more direct and structured relationships between farmers and businesses. For example, a food processing company or large retailer could establish long-term sourcing agreements with small-holder farmers, providing them with a guaranteed market for their crops at fair prices. In return, these businesses could invest in training programs, modern farming inputs, and infrastructure improvements that help farmers increase productivity and reduce post-harvest losses. This mutually beneficial relationship would enable farmers to earn more consistent and higher incomes while ensuring that businesses have access to a reliable supply of locally sourced agricultural products.

One of the key opportunities for local sourcing in Nigeria's agricultural sector lies in the development of value-added industries. Rather than exporting raw agricultural products like cocoa, cashew nuts, or palm oil, Nigeria has the potential to process these products domestically, capturing more of the value chain and creating jobs in agro-processing, packaging, and distribution. For instance, instead of exporting raw cocoa beans, Nigeria could establish chocolate manufacturing facilities, producing finished chocolate products for domestic consumption and export. This approach not only increases the value of agricultural exports but also fosters the development of ancillary industries, such as logistics, marketing, and retail, which further contribute to economic growth.

The development of value-added industries also has the potential to significantly reduce post-harvest losses, a major issue in Nigeria's agricultural supply chain. According to estimates, Nigeria loses between 30% to 40% of its agricultural output due to poor storage, transportation, and processing infrastructure. By investing in local processing facilities, businesses can help ensure that perishable goods, such as fruits, vegetables, and dairy products, are processed and preserved shortly after harvest, reducing waste and increasing the amount of food that reaches consumers. These processing facilities could also serve as hubs for training and innovation, providing farmers with access to modern technologies and practices that improve productivity and sustainability.

Local sourcing in agriculture can also play a crucial role in improving food security in Nigeria. The country currently imports a significant portion of its food, including staples such as rice, wheat, and fish, to meet the needs of its growing population. This reliance on imported food leaves Nigeria vulnerable to global price fluctuations and supply chain disruptions, as seen during the COVID-19 pandemic, when food prices surged due to restrictions on international trade. By promoting local sourcing and investing in domestic agricultural production, Nigeria can reduce its dependence on imports and ensure a more stable and affordable food supply for its population. For example, businesses could prioritize sourcing rice, maize, and other staple crops from local farmers, reducing the need for imports and supporting domestic agricultural development.

In addition to improving food security, local sourcing in agriculture offers opportunities to promote more sustainable and environmentally friendly farming practices. The Nigerian agricultural sector is often characterized by unsustainable practices, such as the overuse of chemical fertilizers, pesticides, and monoculture farming, which can degrade soil health, reduce biodiversity, and contribute to environmental pollution. By working directly with local farmers, businesses can encourage the adoption of sustainable farming techniques, such as agroforestry, crop rotation, organic farming, and water conservation, which help maintain soil fertility, protect natural ecosystems, and reduce the environmental impact of agriculture.

For example, a company sourcing coffee beans from local farmers could invest in training programs that teach farmers how to grow coffee using shade-grown techniques, which not only improve coffee quality but also protect biodiversity and reduce the need for chemical inputs. Similarly, businesses sourcing palm oil could work with farmers to promote sustainable palm oil production practices, reducing deforestation and protecting wildlife habitats. These sustainability efforts can also help businesses meet the growing demand from consumers for ethically produced and environmentally responsible products, creating a competitive advantage in the market.

Furthermore, local sourcing can help foster greater collaboration between businesses, government agencies, and civil society organizations to address the systemic challenges facing Nigeria's agricultural sector. By working together, these stakeholders can develop innovative solutions to improve access to credit for smallholder farmers, enhance infrastructure, and create market linkages that support the growth of local agricultural supply chains. For instance, a public-private partnership could be established to build cold storage facilities in rural areas, providing farmers with the infrastructure they need to reduce post-harvest losses and deliver fresh produce to urban markets.

The role of government is also critical in promoting local sourcing in agriculture. The Nigerian government can play a key role by creating a favorable policy environment that encourages businesses to source locally and invest in the agricultural sector. This could include providing tax incentives, subsidies, or grants for businesses that prioritize local sourcing, as well as investing in infrastructure improvements such as roads, electricity, and telecommunications networks that support agricultural supply chains. Additionally, the government could implement policies that promote sustainable farming practices, such as providing subsidies for organic fertilizers or offering financial support for farmers transitioning to sustainable farming methods.

Finally, local sourcing in agriculture has the potential to contribute to poverty reduction and rural development. Many of Nigeria's rural areas, where smallholder farmers are concentrated, suffer from high levels of poverty, limited access to basic services, and a lack of economic opportunities. By creating stronger market linkages and providing farmers with access to formal supply chains, local sourcing can help bring these communities into the formal economy, improving their livelihoods and contributing to broader rural development. As farmers earn higher incomes and reinvest in their communities, the multiplier effect can lead to improvements in education, healthcare, infrastructure, and overall quality of life in rural areas.

In conclusion, local sourcing presents a transformative opportunity for Nigeria's agricultural sector. By creating more direct relationships between farmers and businesses, developing value-added industries, reducing post-harvest losses, and promoting sustainable farming practices, local sourcing can help improve productivity, enhance food security, and drive economic growth. Moreover, by fostering collaboration between businesses, government, and civil society organizations, local sourcing can address the systemic challenges facing agriculture in Nigeria and contribute to broader rural development. As businesses recognize the benefits of sourcing locally, they have the potential to transform Nigeria's agricultural sector into a more efficient, sustainable, and inclusive engine of economic growth.

CHAPTER 6

MANUFACTURING AND LOCAL SOURCING: BUILDING CAPACITY IN NIGERIA

The manufacturing sector in Nigeria represents a critical pillar of the country's economic growth potential. Despite significant resources and a large labor force, manufacturing remains underdeveloped and often hampered by reliance on imported raw materials, insufficient infrastructure, and high production costs. However, local sourcing offers a promising avenue to revitalize and expand the manufacturing sector. By integrating local suppliers into manufacturing supply chains and reducing dependency on imports, Nigerian manufacturers can lower production costs, improve product quality, and increase competitiveness in both domestic and international markets.

At the heart of local sourcing in manufacturing is the ability to identify and develop raw materials that can be procured within Nigeria. For instance, the textile industry, which historically thrived in Nigeria, has suffered in recent years due to competition from cheaper imported fabrics and a lack of investment in local cotton production. However, with a renewed focus on local sourcing, Nigeria's textile manufacturers can revitalize local cotton farming, reduce import dependency, and rebuild a domestic value chain that encompasses farming, spinning, weaving, and garment production. By sourcing cotton locally, manufacturers can significantly reduce costs tied to importing raw materials, making their products more competitive and fostering job creation across the textile value chain.

The success of the Nigerian cement industry illustrates the potential benefits of local sourcing in manufacturing. By utilizing locally available limestone, Nigerian cement manufacturers such as Dangote Cement have been able to meet domestic demand while reducing reliance on imported materials. This local sourcing strategy has contributed to the growth of the industry, creating jobs and fostering infrastructure development across the country. The model adopted by the cement industry can be applied to other manufacturing sectors, such as steel, chemicals, and plastics, where locally available resources can replace expensive imports, reducing costs and increasing local production capacity.

Local sourcing also contributes to the development of a more robust supply chain ecosystem. As Nigerian manufacturers rely more on local suppliers, they stimulate the growth of related industries. For example, a Nigerian automotive manufacturer sourcing parts locally will drive demand for components such as rubber, glass, or steel, encouraging the development of domestic suppliers. This interconnected supply chain not only strengthens Nigeria's manufacturing base but also builds resilience by reducing dependence on international suppliers.

Moreover, local sourcing in manufacturing presents an opportunity for Nigeria to boost its competitiveness in regional and global markets. By leveraging the advantages of proximity and lower transportation costs, Nigerian manufacturers can produce goods at competitive prices for both domestic consumption and export to neighboring countries. The African Continental Free Trade Area (AfCFTA) agreement further enhances this potential by opening up regional markets and reducing trade barriers across Africa. For Nigerian manufacturers to take full advantage of AfCFTA, a strong local sourcing strategy will be essential, enabling them to scale up production, reduce costs, and compete more effectively in regional supply chains.

Despite the clear benefits, there are significant challenges to integrating local sourcing in Nigeria's manufacturing sector. One of the most pressing challenges is the lack of infrastructure needed to support the reliable delivery of raw materials. Poor road networks, unreliable power supply, and limited access to financing are barriers that prevent local suppliers from scaling up their operations to meet the demands of large manufacturers. Without consistent power and transportation networks, manufacturers face delays in receiving raw materials, which in turn disrupts production schedules and increases costs.

The availability and quality of locally sourced raw materials can also pose challenges to manufacturers. While Nigeria is rich in natural resources, the extraction and processing of these materials are often underdeveloped. For example, sectors such as chemicals and electronics require specialized materials and components that may not yet be produced domestically at the required quality or scale. In these cases, investment in local industries is needed to improve the production capabilities of suppliers, enabling them to meet the stringent quality and volume demands of manufacturing businesses.

Workforce development is another key challenge for local sourcing in manufacturing. For local sourcing to succeed, a skilled labor force capable of handling the technical demands of modern manufacturing processes is essential. Nigerian manufacturers must invest in training programs that equip workers with the skills needed to operate advanced machinery, adhere to quality standards, and optimize production processes. Additionally, partnerships between educational institutions and manufacturing companies can help ensure that graduates are equipped with the practical skills required by the industry, closing the gap between education and employment.

The potential for local sourcing to drive industrial growth in Nigeria is significant. The manufacturing sector, if fully developed, can serve as a major engine of economic diversification, reducing the country's reliance on oil exports and creating a more balanced and resilient economy. By focusing on local sourcing, Nigerian manufacturers can reduce costs, create jobs, and stimulate the growth of related industries, contributing to broader economic development.

Local sourcing also fosters innovation within the manufacturing sector. As manufacturers increasingly rely on local suppliers, there is a growing need for suppliers to develop new technologies, improve production processes, and meet higher quality standards. This demand for innovation creates opportunities for Nigerian businesses to invest in research and development, adopt advanced manufacturing techniques, and build more sophisticated production capabilities. Over time, these innovations will help Nigerian industries become more competitive in both regional and global markets.

In conclusion, local sourcing in manufacturing presents a transformative opportunity for Nigeria. By leveraging local resources, developing domestic suppliers, and investing in workforce development, Nigeria's manufacturing sector can reduce its dependence on imports, improve competitiveness, and drive economic growth. As businesses, governments, and educational institutions work together to address the challenges facing local sourcing, they can unlock the full potential of Nigeria's manufacturing sector and position the country as a hub for industrial production in Africa.

CHAPTER 7

TECHNOLOGY AND INNOVATION: ENABLING LOCAL SOURCING THROUGH DIGITALIZATION

In the 21st century, technology has proven to be a powerful driver of efficiency, growth, and competitiveness across industries. Nowhere is this truer than in supply chain management, where digitalization is revolutionizing how businesses interact with suppliers, manage logistics, and optimize operations. For Nigeria, embracing digital tools and innovation offers a unique opportunity to overcome many of the challenges associated with local sourcing and supply chain inefficiencies. Through digitalization, Nigerian businesses can streamline procurement, improve transparency, foster collaboration, and ensure greater agility in responding to market demands. This chapter explores how technology and innovation can enable local sourcing in Nigeria, empowering industries to unlock the full potential of local supply chains.

One of the most immediate and transformative effects of digitalization on local sourcing is the rise of online platforms and digital marketplaces that connect suppliers and buyers. These platforms provide businesses with access to real-time information about local suppliers, their products, pricing, and availability, allowing for more informed decision-making. In Nigeria, platforms such as TradeDepot and Kobo360 have emerged as critical players in the digitalization of supply chains. TradeDepot, for instance, connects retailers to a network of suppliers, while Kobo360 is transforming logistics by providing an on-demand digital platform for truck transportation. These innovations are streamlining the entire sourcing process, reducing the need for costly intermediaries, and enabling smaller suppliers to access larger markets.

In the agricultural sector, digital platforms have proven especially effective in empowering smallholder farmers by linking them directly to buyers. Platforms like FarmCrowdy and Thrive Agric allow farmers to sell their produce directly to consumers or businesses, eliminating the need for middlemen who often take a significant share of profits. These platforms also provide farmers with vital information on market demand, crop pricing, and best practices in farming, enabling them to make better decisions about what to grow and when to harvest. By connecting farmers to formal supply chains, digital platforms play a pivotal role in promoting local sourcing and enhancing the productivity and income of small-scale producers.

In addition to connecting buyers and suppliers, digitalization brings increased transparency to supply chains. Blockchain technology, for example, is rapidly gaining traction as a tool for ensuring traceability and accountability in sourcing practices. By using blockchain, businesses can track the origin and movement of products throughout the supply chain, from raw material extraction to final delivery. This level of transparency is particularly important in sectors where ethical sourcing and sustainability are major concerns, such as agriculture, mining, and manufacturing. For Nigerian businesses, blockchain can be used to verify that products are sourced locally and produced under environmentally and socially responsible conditions. By providing consumers and buyers with verifiable data, businesses can build trust and credibility, which are essential for long-term success.

Artificial intelligence (AI) and machine learning (ML) are also playing an increasingly important role in optimizing local sourcing strategies. AI-powered tools can analyze vast amounts of data to identify trends, predict demand, and optimize procurement. For example, AI can be used to forecast demand for raw materials, enabling businesses to make more informed decisions about how much to source and when. This helps to reduce overstocking or understocking, ensuring that supply chains are more responsive to fluctuations in demand. In Nigeria's agriculture sector, AI can be used to analyze data on weather patterns, soil conditions, and crop yields, allowing farmers to make better decisions about planting, harvesting, and selling their crops. This data-driven approach improves efficiency and ensures that local sourcing strategies are aligned with actual market needs.

Another significant technological advancement that is transforming supply chain management is the Internet of Things (IoT). IoT devices, such as sensors and RFID tags, allow businesses to monitor the condition and location of products in real-time throughout the supply chain. This is especially valuable for industries dealing with perishable goods, such as food and pharmaceuticals, where maintaining the right conditions during storage and transportation is critical to ensuring product quality. In Nigeria, where infrastructure challenges can cause delays in the transportation of goods, IoT technology can help mitigate these risks by providing businesses with real-time visibility into their supply chains. For example, sensors placed in shipping containers can monitor temperature, humidity, and other environmental conditions, alerting businesses if products are at risk of spoilage.

Logistics is another area where technology is making a significant impact. In Nigeria, poor road networks and traffic congestion can create bottlenecks in the movement of goods, leading to delays and higher transportation costs. However, digital logistics platforms, like Kobo360 and Lori Systems, are helping to optimize transportation routes, improve efficiency, and reduce costs. These platforms use data analytics to match shippers with available truck capacity, ensuring that goods are transported in the most efficient way possible. By improving the efficiency of logistics operations, businesses can reduce lead times, lower transportation costs, and increase the competitiveness of locally sourced products.

Additionally, autonomous vehicles and drones offer exciting new possibilities for overcoming Nigeria's transportation challenges. Autonomous trucks can reduce labor costs and improve the safety and efficiency of road transportation, while drones have the potential to deliver goods to remote or hard-to-reach areas, by passing the country's often underdeveloped road infrastructure. These technologies are still in the early stages of adoption in Nigeria, but they hold significant potential for transforming the logistics landscape and enabling more efficient local sourcing.

The role of big data analytics in supply chain optimization cannot be overstated. With the advent of digitalization, businesses now have access to more data than ever before. However, the challenge lies in making sense of this data and using it to inform decision-making. Big data analytics tools allow businesses to analyze large datasets in real-time, identifying patterns and trends that can help optimize supply chains. For example, a manufacturer sourcing raw materials locally can use big data analytics to monitor supplier performance, track delivery times, and analyze pricing trends. This information enables the manufacturer to make more informed sourcing decisions, improve supplier relationships, and reduce costs.

While the benefits of digitalization are clear, there are several challenges that Nigeria must address to fully realize the potential of technology in local sourcing. One of the most significant barriers is the lack of reliable internet access, particularly in rural areas where many local suppliers are based. Without access to digital tools and platforms, these suppliers may struggle to participate in the digital economy, limiting their ability to benefit from local sourcing opportunities. Expanding broadband access and improving internet connectivity will be critical for ensuring that all businesses, regardless of location, can leverage the advantages of digitalization.

Another challenge is the need for digital literacy and skills development. As supply chains become increasingly digitized, businesses will need employees who are capable of using and managing these technologies effectively. However, many workers in Nigeria lack the necessary digital skills to operate in a tech-driven supply chain environment. Investing in education and training programs that focus on digital literacy, data analysis, and technology management will be essential for building a workforce that can support the digital transformation of supply chains.

To overcome these challenges, public-private partnerships (PPPs) will play a key role in driving the digitalization of Nigeria's supply chains. By collaborating with the private sector, the government can invest in the infrastructure and training needed to support digitalization. For example, PPPs could be established to expand internet access in rural areas, provide digital literacy training to workers, or develop technology hubs that foster innovation in supply chain management.

In conclusion, technology and innovation are critical enablers of local sourcing in Nigeria. From digital platforms that connect buyers and suppliers to AI and IoT tools that optimize procurement and logistics, digitalization is transforming how businesses manage their supply chains. By embracing these technologies, Nigerian businesses can improve efficiency, reduce costs, and increase the competitiveness of locally sourced products. However, to fully realize the benefits of digitalization, Nigeria must address challenges related to internet access, digital literacy, and infrastructure. Through investments in technology, education, and public-private partnerships, Nigeria can build the digital supply chains of the future, driving economic growth, job creation, and sustainable development.

CHAPTER 8

INFRASTRUCTURAL BOTTLENECKS: CHALLENGES TO SCALING LOCAL SUPPLY CHAINS

In any economy, infrastructure is the foundation upon which efficient and effective supply chains are built. From roads and ports to energy and telecommunications networks, infrastructure plays a vital role in determining how goods are produced, transported, and delivered. In Nigeria, however, inadequate infrastructure has long been one of the most significant impediments to the growth and development of local supply chains. While local sourcing presents a promising strategy for strengthening Nigeria's economy, scaling these initiatives will require addressing the country's infrastructural bottlenecks. This chapter explores the key infrastructure challenges facing local supply chains in Nigeria and examines potential solutions for overcoming these obstacles.

One of the most pressing infrastructural challenges in Nigeria is the state of the country's transportation networks. Roads, railways, and ports form the backbone of any supply chain, enabling the movement of goods from suppliers to manufacturers, distributors, and consumers. However, Nigeria's road network, in particular, is in poor condition, with many key highways and rural roads suffering from neglect, underdevelopment, and congestion. This significantly increases transportation costs and delays, making it difficult for local suppliers to deliver goods on time and at competitive prices.

Rural areas, where many of Nigeria's agricultural producers are located, are particularly affected by poor transportation infrastructure. Smallholder farmers often struggle to transport their produce to urban markets or processing facilities, resulting in high levels of post-harvest losses. Improving rural road networks would not only reduce transportation costs for these farmers but also increase their market access, enabling them to participate more fully in local supply chains.

In addition to roads, Nigeria's rail network has long been underutilized as a mode of freight transport. Railways offer a more efficient and cost-effective means of transporting large volumes of goods over long distances compared to road transport. However, decades of underinvestment have left much of Nigeria's rail infrastructure in a state of disrepair. Recent efforts to modernize the rail system offer hope for improving freight transportation, but significant investment is still needed to expand the rail network and integrate it more fully into Nigeria's supply chains.

Ports also play a critical role in Nigeria's supply chains, particularly for businesses that rely on imports and exports. However, Nigeria's major ports, such as the Apapa and Tin Can Island ports in Lagos, suffer from severe congestion and inefficiencies, leading to long delays and high costs for businesses. These challenges are compounded by bureaucratic bottlenecks, such as customs procedures, which further slowdown the movement of goods. Addressing these issues will be essential for improving the overall efficiency of Nigeria's supply chains and enabling local suppliers to compete more effectively in both domestic and international markets.

Energy infrastructure is another critical challenge for local sourcing in Nigeria. The country's power grid is notoriously unreliable, with frequent blackouts and power shortages disrupting business operations across industries. This lack of reliable energy forces many businesses to rely on costly diesel generators, significantly increasing production costs. For local suppliers, especially small and medium-sized enterprises (SMEs), the high cost of energy can be prohibitive, limiting their ability to scale up production and meet the demands of larger supply chains.

Improving Nigeria's energy infrastructure is essential for reducing production costs and enabling local suppliers to compete more effectively. Investments in renewable energy sources, such as solar and wind power, could provide more reliable and sustainable energy solutions, particularly in rural areas that are not connected to the national grid. Additionally, efforts to modernize and expand the country's power grid would help ensure that businesses have access to the energy they need to operate efficiently.

Communication infrastructure also plays a key role in enabling efficient supply chains. In today's digital economy, businesses rely on high-speed internet and communication networks to manage their operations, coordinate with suppliers, and reach customers. However, many parts of Nigeria, particularly rural areas, lack access to reliable internet connectivity, limiting the ability of local suppliers to participate in digital supply chains. Expanding broadband access and improving the country's telecommunications infrastructure will be critical for enabling local sourcing and ensuring that suppliers can take advantage of digital tools and platforms.

Infrastructural bottlenecks not only affect the movement of goods but also hinder the development of human capital. Access to quality education, healthcare, and other essential services is limited in many parts of Nigeria due to poor infrastructure. This has a direct impact on the availability of skilled labor for local supply chains, as workers in underserved areas may lack the training and resources needed to meet the demands of modern industries. Improving infrastructure in these areas would not only benefit local suppliers but also contribute to the broader development of Nigeria's economy by creating a more skilled and capable workforce.

While addressing Nigeria's infrastructural challenges is a long-term effort that requires significant investment, there are steps that businesses and policymakers can take in the short term to mitigate the impact of these bottlenecks on local sourcing. For example, businesses can collaborate with local governments and community organizations to invest in small-scale infrastructure projects, such as building feeder roads or installing solar panels for local suppliers. Additionally, public-private partnerships can play a key role in financing and implementing larger infrastructure projects, such as upgrading transportation networks or expanding access to electricity.

Another important strategy for overcoming infrastructural bottlenecks is the use of technology to optimize logistics and supply chain management. For example, businesses can use GPS tracking and route optimization software to improve the efficiency of transportation routes, reducing delays and minimizing the impact of poor road conditions. Similarly, digital platforms can help suppliers manage their inventory more effectively, ensuring that they can meet demand even when faced with logistical challenges.

In the long term, addressing Nigeria's infrastructural bottlenecks will be essential for scaling local sourcing and building more resilient supply chains. By investing in transportation, energy, and communication infrastructure, Nigeria can unlock the full potential of its local suppliers, enabling them to compete more effectively in both domestic and international markets. These investments will not only improve the efficiency of local supply chains but also contribute to broader economic development, creating jobs, reducing poverty, and improving the quality of life for millions of Nigerians.

As Nigeria looks to the future, overcoming its infrastructural challenges will be key to ensuring that local sourcing can play a central role in the country's economic development. By addressing these bottlenecks, Nigeria can build stronger, more efficient supply chains that support local businesses, create jobs, and drive sustainable growth. Through a combination of government action, private sector investment, and technological innovation, Nigeria can transform its infrastructure and build the foundation for a more prosperous and resilient economy.

CHAPTER 9

GOVERNMENT POLICIES AND LOCAL SOURCING: ANALYZING THE ROLE OF POLICY FRAMEWORKS

Government policy is central to shaping the direction and success of local sourcing initiatives in any economy. In Nigeria, the government's role in encouraging local sourcing is crucial for overcoming the country's numerous challenges related to import dependence, underdeveloped industries, and economic vulnerability. A comprehensive and coherent policy framework can create a conducive environment for businesses to source locally, while also fostering the growth of domestic industries, stimulating employment, and advancing the nation's broader economic development goals.

Historically, Nigeria's economic policies have been inconsistent, particularly regarding trade, industrialization, and economic development. Much of Nigeria's industrial and economic strategy since independence has been driven by a focus on foreign direct investment (FDI) and reliance on imports to meet the country's needs. This import dependence has often stifled local production and created significant trade imbalances, while also making the economy vulnerable to global commodity price fluctuations, exchange rate volatility, and external economic shocks. Nigeria's overreliance on imported goods, especially in industries like manufacturing, has limited the development of domestic industries and constrained the potential of local suppliers.

To address these challenges, the Nigerian government has in recent years implemented several policy measures aimed at promoting local content and import substitution. These strategies are designed to encourage local sourcing, reduce dependence on imports, and build domestic industrial capacity. One of the most significant policy initiatives in this regard is the Nigerian Oil and Gas Industry Content Development Act of 2010, which mandated the use of local resources and labor in the country's oil and gas sector. The law required foreign companies operating in Nigeria to prioritize the use of Nigerian goods and services wherever possible, with the goal of increasing the participation of local businesses in the sector.

The success of the Nigerian Content Act in the oil and gas sector has shown the potential for similar policies to be applied in other sectors of the economy. By expanding local content requirements to industries such as agriculture, manufacturing, and technology, the Nigerian government can encourage businesses to source more of their materials, labor, and services from local suppliers. For example, local content policies in the agricultural sector could require food processors to source a minimum percentage of their raw materials from Nigerian farmers, while in the technology sector, companies could be incentivized to use Nigerian software developers and tech professionals.

However, while local content policies have had a positive impact on the oil and gas sector, there are several challenges to replicating this success in other industries. One key issue is the need for robust enforcement mechanisms to ensure compliance with local content requirements. In some cases, businesses have circumvented local content regulations by engaging in tokenistic practices, such as subcontracting small portions of their work to local companies while continuing to rely heavily on foreign suppliers. Effective monitoring and enforcement of local content policies are critical for ensuring that businesses genuinely engage with and invest in local suppliers.

In addition to local content policies, the Nigerian government has also embraced import substitution as a strategy for reducing the country's dependence on foreign goods. Import substitution policies typically involve the imposition of tariffs, quotas, or outright bans on certain imported goods, with the aim of encouraging local production. By making imports more expensive or less accessible, these policies create an incentive for businesses to source locally or invest in domestic manufacturing.

One of the most notable examples of import substitution in Nigeria is the government's push to boost local rice production by banning rice imports and offering incentives to local rice farmers. This policy has been largely successful in increasing domestic rice production, with Nigeria emerging as one of the largest rice producers in Africa. However, import substitution policies must be implemented carefully to avoid unintended consequences, such as inflation or shortages of essential goods. In some cases, protectionist policies can lead to price increases for consumers if local producers are unable to meet demand or if their products are significantly more expensive than imported alternatives.

To support local sourcing and import substitution, the Nigerian government has also launched several initiatives aimed at industrial development and economic diversification. Two key policy frameworks in this regard are the National Industrial Revolution Plan (NIRP) and the Economic Recovery and Growth Plan (ERGP). Both initiatives emphasize the need to build a competitive industrial base, promote local production, and diversify the economy away from its dependence on oil revenues. The NIRP focuses on key sectors such as agriculture, manufacturing, and solid minerals, while the ERGP outlines strategies for achieving sustainable growth through investment in infrastructure, human capital development, and innovation.

For these policies to be successful, they must be backed by sustained political will, adequate funding, and effective implementation. One of the challenges Nigeria has faced in the past is the disconnect between policy formulation and execution. Policies that look good on paper often fail to achieve their desired outcomes due to lack of coordination among government agencies, inconsistent enforcement, or insufficient funding. Ensuring that local sourcing policies are implemented effectively will require close collaboration between the federal government, state governments, and the private sector.

State and local governments also have a critical role to play in promoting local sourcing. Given Nigeria's vast size and regional diversity, a one-size-fits-all approach to local sourcing is unlikely to be effective. State governments can tailor their policies to their specific economic conditions, focusing on industries where they have a competitive advantage. For example, states with rich agricultural resources may prioritize policies that promote local sourcing in food production and agro-processing, while states with a strong industrial base may focus on developing local manufacturing and technology sectors.

Public procurement policies are another tool that the Nigerian government can use to support local sourcing. By prioritizing the use of locally produced goods and services in government contracts, the government can create a stable market for local suppliers and encourage them to invest in expanding their operations and improving the quality of their products. Government projects in sectors such as infrastructure, education, and healthcare present significant opportunities for local suppliers to participate in formal supply chains and contribute to economic development.

Beyond setting policies and regulations, the government can also play a role in fostering public-private partnerships (PPPs) that bring together the resources and expertise of both the public and private sectors. PPPs can be particularly effective in addressing infrastructural challenges that limit the growth of local supply chains, such as inadequate roads, power supply, or logistics facilities. For example, partnerships between the government and private companies can be used to build critical infrastructure, such as industrial parks, processing facilities, or power plants, which are necessary for supporting the efficient operation of supply chains.

Access to financing is another area where government intervention is needed to support local sourcing. Many local suppliers, particularly small and medium-sized enterprises (SMEs), struggle to access the capital needed to scale their operations and meet the demands of larger businesses. Government-backed credit schemes, grants, and incentives can help bridge this financing gap, allowing local suppliers to invest in new equipment, expand production capacity, and improve their competitiveness. Additionally, government agencies can work with financial institutions to develop tailored financing products that meet the specific needs of local suppliers, such as low-interest loans, microfinance options, or export financing for businesses looking to enter international markets.

Regulatory reforms are also essential for creating an enabling environment for local sourcing. In Nigeria, bureaucratic red tape, corruption, and inconsistent enforcement of regulations can create significant obstacles for businesses. Streamlining regulatory processes, improving transparency, and reducing the administrative burden on businesses can help create a more business-friendly environment that encourages investment in local industries. For example, simplifying the process for registering new businesses, obtaining permits, and accessing government incentives can reduce barriers to entry for local suppliers, making it easier for them to compete in formal supply chains.

Education and workforce development policies are also critical for supporting local sourcing. As industries grow and local suppliers take on more prominent roles in supply chains, there will be a greater demand for skilled workers who can meet the technical and operational needs of these industries. The government can play a key role in addressing the skills gap by investing in vocational training, apprenticeship programs, and partnerships with educational institutions to ensure that workers are equipped with the knowledge and skills needed to succeed in the evolving economy.

Trade policy is another area where government intervention is crucial for promoting local sourcing. While it is important for Nigeria to protect and support its local industries, it is equally important to remain integrated into the global economy. Nigeria's trade policies should strike a balance between encouraging local production and maintaining access to global markets, ensuring that Nigerian businesses can compete internationally while also benefiting from opportunities for export growth. Trade agreements, such as the African Continental Free Trade Area (AfCFTA), present significant opportunities for Nigerian businesses to expand into regional markets and build more resilient supply chains.

In conclusion, government policies play a fundamental role in shaping the future of local sourcing in Nigeria. By adopting a comprehensive and coordinated approach that addresses the unique challenges faced by local suppliers, the Nigerian government can help create an enabling environment for local sourcing to thrive. This will require sustained investment in infrastructure, regulatory reforms, and support for workforce development, as well as close collaboration between the public and private sectors. If implemented effectively, these policies can unlock the full potential of local sourcing, contributing to a more resilient, self-sufficient, and prosperous Nigerian economy.

CHAPTER 10

CASE STUDIES: SUCCESSFUL LOCAL SOURCING IN NIGERIAN BUSINESSES

Nigeria's economy is increasingly embracing the concept of local sourcing as businesses across different sectors begin to realize the benefits of building resilient and sustainable supply chains that rely on domestic suppliers. By integrating local sourcing practices, these businesses have improved their competitiveness, reduced costs, and strengthened relationships with local communities. In this chapter, we will explore several case studies of Nigerian businesses that have successfully implemented local sourcing strategies, examining the key drivers of their success, the challenges they faced, and the lessons learned from their experiences.

One of the most prominent success stories in local sourcing in Nigeria is the rise of the Dangote Group, a conglomerate with interests in cement, sugar, salt, and oil. Dangote Cement, in particular, stands out as a prime example of how local sourcing can drive industrial growth. By utilizing locally sourced limestone, Dangote Cement has reduced its reliance on imported raw materials, significantly lowering production costs and increasing profitability. The company's investment in local resources has allowed it to dominate the Nigerian cement market, supplying both the domestic market and exporting to neighboring countries. In addition to reducing the country's reliance on imported cement, Dangote Cement has created thousands of jobs for Nigerians, contributing to the broader goal of economic development.

The success of Dangote Cement can be attributed to several key factors. First, the company's decision to invest in local sourcing was driven by a clear understanding of the economic and logistical advantages of using domestically available resources. By sourcing limestone locally, Dangote was able to reduce transportation costs, improve production efficiency, and mitigate the risks associated with global supply chain disruptions. Second, the company's commitment to investing in local infrastructure, such as building cement plants in strategic locations, helped to ensure a steady and reliable supply of raw materials. Finally, Dangote Cement's success is a testament to the importance of government support and favorable policy frameworks, including import restrictions on cement that encouraged local production.

Another notable example of successful local sourcing is Innoson Vehicle Manufacturing (IVM), Nigeria's first indigenous car manufacturer. Innoson has embraced local sourcing by producing a significant portion of its vehicle components domestically, including seats, plastic parts, and body panels. By working closely with local suppliers, Innoson has been able to reduce its production costs, customize its vehicles to meet the specific needs of the Nigerian market, and offer affordable transportation options to consumers. The company's success highlights the potential for local sourcing to drive innovation in Nigeria's manufacturing sector, as well as the importance of building strong partnerships between manufacturers and local suppliers.

One of the key challenges that Innoson has faced in its local sourcing efforts is the limited availability of certain high-tech components, such as engines and electronics, which are not yet produced domestically. To address this challenge, the company has pursued a hybrid strategy, sourcing these components internationally while continuing to invest in the development of local suppliers for other parts of the production process. This approach has allowed Innoson to remain competitive in the Nigerian automotive market while also contributing to the growth of the local manufacturing ecosystem.

In the agricultural sector, Olam Nigeria stands out as a leader in promoting local sourcing. Olam, a global agribusiness company, has made significant investments in Nigeria's rice production value chain, sourcing rice locally from smallholder farmers and operating large-scale rice farms and milling facilities. Olam's investment in local rice production has helped to reduce Nigeria's reliance on imported rice, improve food security, and create economic opportunities for rural communities. By working closely with smallholder farmers, Olam has provided farmers with access to high-quality inputs, training, and market access, helping them to improve their productivity and incomes.

The success of Olam's local sourcing strategy can be attributed to the company's long-term commitment to building sustainable and inclusive agricultural supply chains. Olam has invested in the development of infrastructure, such as irrigation systems and milling facilities, to ensure a reliable supply of rice from local farmers. The company has also focused on building strong relationships with its suppliers, providing them with the support and resources they need to succeed. This collaborative approach has not only benefited Olam but has also contributed to the broader development of Nigeria's agricultural sector, creating a more resilient and productive supply chain.

In the technology sector, Andela is an example of a Nigerian company that has successfully embraced local talent sourcing to build a global business. Andela identifies and trains software developers across Africa, connecting them with international clients who need skilled tech talent. By investing in the local human capital, Andela has created a pipeline of highly skilled workers who can compete in the global marketplace. The company's success demonstrates the potential for Nigeria to become a hub for digital talent, with local sourcing of skilled labor serving as a key driver of growth in the technology sector.

Andela's success can be attributed to its innovative business model, which focuses on developing local talent and providing them with the skills and opportunities needed to succeed in the global tech industry. By partnering with local universities, offering rigorous training programs, and leveraging technology to connect Nigerian developers with international clients, Andela has been able to create a scalable and sustainable talent sourcing platform. The company's ability to tap into the growing demand for tech talent, both in Nigeria and abroad, has allowed it to expand rapidly and establish itself as a leader in the African tech industry.

Another successful example of local sourcing in the technology sector is Zinox Technologies, a Nigerian company that manufactures computers and ICT equipment. Zinox has built its business by sourcing components locally and assembling its products in Nigeria, allowing the company to reduce costs, offer competitive pricing, and provide high-quality tech products to the Nigerian market. By focusing on local manufacturing, Zinox has created jobs, supported the growth of Nigeria's ICT sector, and positioned itself as a leader in digital innovation in Africa.

In the food and beverage industry, Nigerian Breweries has embraced local sourcing by working with Nigerian farmers to source key ingredients, such as sorghum and cassava. By investing in local agriculture, the company has reduced its reliance on imported barley and helped to create a sustainable supply chain that supports Nigerian farmers. This approach has enabled Nigerian Breweries to reduce production costs, improve product availability, and support the livelihoods of local farmers. The company's success demonstrates how local sourcing can be integrated into supply chains in ways that benefit both businesses and communities.

These case studies illustrate the diverse ways in which Nigerian businesses are leveraging local sourcing to drive growth, innovation, and competitiveness. From manufacturing and agriculture to technology and food production, local sourcing has proven to be a powerful strategy for building resilient supply chains and fostering economic development. By investing in local resources, collaborating with local suppliers, and developing the skills of the Nigerian workforce, these businesses have not only improved their own operations but also contributed to the broader development of Nigeria's economy.

The common thread across these success stories is the willingness of these businesses to invest in long-term relationships with local suppliers and communities. Local sourcing is not just about reducing costs or complying with government policies, it is about creating sustainable partnerships that benefit both businesses and the broader economy. These companies have demonstrated that local sourcing can be a win-win strategy, providing businesses with the resources and flexibility they need to succeed while also creating jobs, supporting local industries, and driving economic development.

As more Nigerian businesses adopt local sourcing practices, the potential for further growth and development in the country's supply chains is immense. By learning from the experiences of successful companies, businesses across Nigeria can unlock new opportunities for innovation, competitiveness, and sustainability, contributing to the long-term prosperity of the nation.

CHAPTER 11

SUSTAINABILITY AND LOCAL SOURCING: THE ENVIRONMENTAL BENEFITS

In recent years, the world has shifted its focus toward sustainability, with businesses and consumers alike increasingly conscious of the environmental impact of their choices. As part of this global trend, supply chains have come under scrutiny for their contribution to pollution, resource depletion, and climate change. For Nigeria, where environmental challenges such as deforestation, pollution, and the effects of climate change are pressing concerns, local sourcing offers a powerful solution for reducing environmental impact while promoting economic growth. Local sourcing encourages the use of nearby resources, reduces transportation emissions, and fosters sustainable production practices critical components for building a greener, more resilient economy.

One of the most direct environmental benefits of local sourcing is the reduction of transportation-related emissions. In globalized supply chains, goods often travel across continents by sea, air, and land, consuming vast amounts of fuel and contributing to significant greenhouse gas emissions. Transportation accounts for a large proportion of the carbon footprint associated with the movement of goods. Local sourcing, however, allows businesses to source products, raw materials, and components closer to home, minimizing the need for long-distance transportation. In Nigeria, this shift could lead to a significant reduction in emissions as businesses depend less on importing materials and more on local suppliers. By shortening supply chains and decreasing reliance on fossil fuel-powered transportation, Nigeria can make meaningful progress in its efforts to combat climate change.

Beyond reducing emissions, local sourcing encourages the responsible use of locally available natural resources. Nigeria is a country rich in agriculture, minerals, and natural raw materials, many of which can be sourced sustainably if managed correctly. Rather than relying on foreign imports, which are often produced under less environmentally friendly conditions, Nigeria can capitalize on its domestic resources in a way that protects local ecosystems. For example, sourcing timber from sustainably managed local forests could help reduce deforestation while promoting responsible forestry practices. This model can be extended to various industries—whether it's the use of sustainably farmed palm oil or locally extracted minerals in manufacturing—allowing Nigeria to maintain a balance between economic development and environmental conservation.

The environmental advantages of local sourcing extend into the realm of sustainable farming practices. Nigeria's agricultural sector, which employs a large portion of the population, can be transformed by promoting smaller-scale, diversified farming systems that rely on traditional knowledge and less intensive farming methods. Industrialized agriculture, which relies heavily on monocultures, chemical inputs, and mechanization, often leads to land degradation, soil depletion, and the loss of biodiversity. Local sourcing can counter this by encouraging businesses to work with smallholder farmers who use sustainable practices such as crop rotation, agroforestry, and organic farming. These methods not only preserve the health of the land but also reduce the environmental impact associated with the production of food and raw materials.

Sustainability in local sourcing is not limited to agriculture. In manufacturing, local sourcing can encourage more sustainable production processes by incentivizing businesses to work closely with suppliers who prioritize environmental stewardship. Local suppliers often have a vested interest in maintaining the long-term viability of their resources, as they rely on local ecosystems for their livelihoods. Businesses that source locally can collaborate with these suppliers to implement cleaner production techniques, reduce waste, and promote the responsible use of energy and materials. For instance, a Nigerian textile manufacturer might work with local cotton farmers to adopt water-efficient irrigation practices or minimize the use of harmful pesticides. This kind of collaboration can help drive environmental improvements throughout the supply chain.

The concept of the circular economy is also closely tied to local sourcing. A circular economy emphasizes reducing waste, reusing materials, and recycling products to extend their lifecycle. Local sourcing can play a pivotal role in supporting circular economy initiatives by promoting the use of locally sourced materials that are easier to recycle or repurpose within the local economy. For example, a local plastics manufacturer could source recycled plastics from domestic recycling facilities, reducing the demand for new plastic production and keeping waste within the loop. This approach not only reduces environmental harm but also creates new economic opportunities in recycling, refurbishment, and sustainable product design.

Furthermore, the environmental benefits of local sourcing extend to water conservation and air quality. In Nigeria, where many regions face water scarcity, businesses that source locally can help minimize water usage by working with suppliers who prioritize water-efficient production methods. This is especially relevant in agriculture, where local farmers can use traditional irrigation techniques that conserve water and preserve soil moisture. Local sourcing can also reduce air pollution by limiting the need for long-distance transportation of goods, which often involves heavy trucks and ships emitting pollutants that degrade air quality.

In the agricultural sector, local sourcing supports the use of sustainable, low-impact farming practices that reduce the environmental footprint of food production. Industrial agriculture is often associated with the overuse of fertilizers, pesticides, and heavy machinery, all of which can harm ecosystems. In contrast, smallholder farmers in Nigeria frequently employ more sustainable methods that align with the country's environmental conditions. Practices such as intercropping, agroforestry, and using organic fertilizers help maintain soil health, conserve biodiversity, and protect water sources. By sourcing agricultural products from these farmers, businesses contribute to preserving the environment and protecting rural livelihoods.

Local sourcing also addresses another key environmental challenge: waste management. The rise of consumerism has led to a surge in waste production, much of which ends up in landfills or polluting natural environments. By promoting local production and consumption, Nigeria can adopt more effective waste management strategies, including recycling, composting, and repurposing waste materials. This, in turn, can reduce the amount of waste that ends up polluting rivers, oceans, and land ecosystems.

While the environmental benefits of local sourcing are clear, ensuring that these benefits are fully realized requires a concerted effort from businesses, governments, and communities. One of the main challenges is the lack of reliable data and transparency regarding the environmental impact of local supply chains. Without accurate data on emissions, resource use, and waste generation, it is difficult for businesses to assess the sustainability of their sourcing practices. Technologies such as blockchain, which provides a secure and transparent ledger of transactions, can help address this challenge by offering real-time tracking of environmental indicators throughout the supply chain. By leveraging such technologies, businesses can monitor the sustainability of their suppliers and make more informed decisions about their sourcing strategies.

Collaboration is another critical factor in promoting sustainable local sourcing. Businesses must work closely with suppliers, governments, and non-governmental organizations (NGOs) to ensure that environmental standards are met throughout the supply chain. Public-private partnerships (PPPs) can play a pivotal role in fostering sustainable practices, with governments providing the regulatory frameworks and financial incentives needed to encourage businesses to adopt greener practices. NGOs and community organizations can also help by offering training and support to local suppliers on sustainable farming, forestry, and manufacturing techniques.

Government policies and regulations are essential for promoting sustainability in local sourcing. By setting clear environmental standards and offering incentives for businesses that adopt sustainable practices, the Nigerian government can play a crucial role in driving the transition to a more sustainable economy. For example, implementing stricter regulations on deforestation, water usage, and carbon emissions can help ensure that local suppliers meet environmental goals. At the same time, offering tax breaks, subsidies, or grants to businesses that invest in sustainability can provide the financial support needed to scale up these initiatives.

The role of consumers in promoting sustainable local sourcing should not be overlooked. As awareness of environmental issues grows, consumers are increasingly demanding products that are ethically sourced and produced with minimal environmental impact. Businesses that prioritize sustainability in their sourcing practices can tap into this growing market by offering products that meet these consumer preferences. This trend is particularly evident in sectors such as food, fashion, and consumer goods, where environmentally conscious consumers are willing to pay a premium for products that align with their values.

In conclusion, local sourcing offers a powerful solution to many of the environmental challenges facing Nigeria today. By reducing transportation emissions, promoting the sustainable use of local resources, and encouraging environmentally responsible production practices, local sourcing can play a critical role in building a greener, more resilient economy. However, realizing the full potential of local sourcing will require collaboration between businesses, governments, and communities, as well as a commitment to transparency, innovation, and continuous improvement. As Nigeria continues to develop its local supply chains, sustainability must remain at the forefront of these efforts, ensuring that economic growth is balanced with environmental protection for future generations.

CHAPTER 12

FINANCING LOCAL SUPPLY CHAINS: ACCESS TO CREDIT AND INVESTMENT

One of the most significant obstacles to the growth and scaling of local supply chains in Nigeria is the lack of access to adequate financing. For small and medium-sized enterprises (SMEs), which form the backbone of Nigeria's local economy, securing the necessary capital to expand operations, purchase equipment, or hire additional labor can be incredibly challenging. This issue is particularly pronounced in industries like agriculture and manufacturing, where initial investments can be substantial, and returns take time to materialize. Without sufficient financial support, many local suppliers are unable to scale their operations to meet the demands of larger supply chains, preventing them from competing effectively with international suppliers.

Access to finance is crucial to the success of local sourcing initiatives, and yet, many local businesses face significant barriers when seeking funding. Traditional banks and financial institutions often view SMEs as high-risk borrowers. These businesses may lack formal credit histories, sufficient collateral, or the consistent revenue streams that banks typically require for loan approval. Additionally, SMEs in Nigeria are often disproportionately affected by economic volatility, regulatory uncertainty, and infrastructural challenges, all of which contribute to the perception of risk. As a result, many local suppliers are unable to secure the loans, lines of credit, or investments they need to grow.

To address these challenges, it is essential to develop financing solutions tailored to the specific needs of local suppliers and SMEs. One such solution is microfinance, which has become a critical source of funding for many small businesses in Nigeria. Microfinance institutions (MFIs) provide small-scale loans to businesses that may not qualify for traditional bank loans, offering more flexible terms and less stringent collateral requirements. MFIs have proven particularly effective in rural areas and among informal businesses, which are often underserved by traditional financial institutions. By offering smaller, more accessible loans, MFIs enable local suppliers to invest in their operations, purchase raw materials, and scale up production to meet demand.

Another innovative approach to financing local supply chains is the rise of crowdfunding and peer-to-peer (P2P) lending platforms. These platforms allow businesses to raise capital directly from individual investors, by passing the traditional banking system. In Nigeria, platforms like Farmcrowdy have emerged as successful models for connecting smallholder farmers with investors who are interested in supporting local agriculture. These platforms not only provide farmers with the capital they need to invest in seeds, fertilizers, and equipment, but also create a sense of community and shared ownership in the success of local enterprises. By enabling direct investment in local supply chains, crowdfunding and P2P lending platforms can help unlock new sources of capital for SMEs, particularly in sectors like agriculture and manufacturing.

Government-backed credit schemes and development finance institutions (DFIs) also play an essential role in financing local supply chains. In Nigeria, institutions like the Bank of Industry (BOI) and the Nigerian Export-Import Bank (NEXIM) have been established to provide financial support to businesses that contribute to the country's economic development. These institutions offer low-interest loans, grants, and credit guarantees to businesses involved in sectors such as manufacturing, agriculture, and export-oriented industries. For example, the BOI's SME Loan Scheme offers financing at favorable rates to small businesses, helping them invest in new machinery, expand production capacity, and create jobs. By providing targeted financial support, these institutions can help level the playing field for local suppliers and promote the growth of domestic supply chains.

In addition to government-backed financing, public-private partnerships (PPPs) present a valuable opportunity for funding local supply chain development. Through PPPs, the government can collaborate with private investors to finance large-scale infrastructure projects that are essential for supporting local suppliers. For instance, partnerships between the government and private companies could be used to build cold storage facilities, processing plants, or logistics hubs in rural areas. These investments would not only improve the efficiency of local supply chains but also reduce post-harvest losses and ensure that locally sourced products reach consumers in good condition.

Impact investing is another financing mechanism that has gained traction in recent years. Impact investors seek to generate both financial returns and positive social or environmental outcomes through their investments. In the context of local sourcing, impact investors can provide capital to businesses that prioritize sustainability, support local communities, or promote economic inclusion. By investing in companies that source materials locally or work closely with local suppliers, impact investors can help create a more resilient and equitable economy while also achieving their financial objectives.

Supply chain financing (SCF) is an additional option for local suppliers looking to manage cash flow and secure working capital. SCF allows businesses to access funds based on their accounts receivable or inventory, providing immediate liquidity without the need for traditional loans. In a typical SCF arrangement, a buyer agrees to pay a supplier's invoice early, with a financial institution providing the necessary funds upfront. This arrangement benefits both the supplier, who receives immediate payment, and the buyer, who may be able to negotiate better terms or discounts in exchange for early payment. SCF can be particularly beneficial for local suppliers working with larger companies, as it helps them bridge cash flow gaps and maintain a steady production cycle.

In addition to SCF, trade credit is another important tool for local suppliers looking to manage their finances. Trade credit allows suppliers to receive goods or services from their own suppliers on credit, with the agreement to pay at a later date. This arrangement can help local businesses preserve their working capital and invest in other areas of their operations, such as hiring additional staff or purchasing new equipment. However, trade credit requires a high degree of trust between buyers and suppliers, making it essential for local businesses to build strong, long-term relationships with their partners.

While access to financing is crucial for the success of local sourcing initiatives, it is equally important for businesses to develop sound financial management practices. Many local suppliers, particularly SMEs, may lack the financial literacy or expertise needed to manage their finances effectively. To address this challenge, governments, financial institutions, and development organizations can offer financial literacy programs, training workshops, and mentorship initiatives that help local businesses develop the skills they need to secure financing, manage cash flow, and grow sustainably. For example, training programs could teach local suppliers how to prepare financial statements, create detailed business plans, and track their expenses and revenues.

Digital financial platforms, such as mobile banking and digital wallets, are also transforming the way local suppliers access capital and manage their finances. In many parts of Africa, including Nigeria, mobile money services like M-Pesa have revolutionized financial inclusion by providing individuals and businesses with a convenient and secure way to save, transfer, and borrow money. By expanding the availability of digital financial services in Nigeria, local suppliers can gain easier access to credit, make payments more efficiently, and improve their overall financial management.

The role of the government in promoting financial inclusion and supporting local sourcing initiatives cannot be overstated. Governments can create an enabling environment for local suppliers by implementing policies that encourage lending to SMEs, offering tax incentives to businesses that invest in local supply chains, and reducing bureaucratic barriers to accessing credit. Additionally, governments can establish credit guarantee schemes that reduce the risk for banks and financial institutions, making them more willing to lend to small businesses.

Collaboration between the public and private sectors is essential for ensuring that local suppliers have access to the financing they need to grow and thrive. By working together, governments, financial institutions, and private investors can develop innovative financing solutions that support the growth of local supply chains while promoting economic inclusion, job creation, and sustainable development.

In conclusion, access to financing is one of the most significant challenges facing local suppliers in Nigeria's supply chains. However, with the right mix of financial products, government support, and public-private collaboration, these challenges can be overcome. By providing local suppliers with the capital, they need to scale their operations, invest in innovation, and compete in both domestic and international markets, Nigeria can unlock the full potential of its local supply chains. This, in turn, will contribute to the broader goals of economic diversification, poverty reduction, and sustainable growth.

CHAPTER 13

PUBLIC-PRIVATE PARTNERSHIPS: COLLABORATING FOR SUPPLY CHAIN SUCCESS

Public-private partnerships (PPPs) are a vital tool for advancing local sourcing and strengthening Nigeria's supply chains. These collaborations between government entities and private businesses leverage the strengths of both sectors to address challenges such as infrastructure deficits, financing gaps, and workforce shortages, which often impede the scaling of local suppliers. In the context of local sourcing, PPPs create synergies that benefit not only businesses and governments but also communities and the broader economy.

One of the keyways PPPs can support local sourcing is through infrastructure development. Nigeria's infrastructure particularly its transportation networks, energy supply, and logistics facilities remains underdeveloped, posing significant obstacles to the efficient operation of local supply chains. Roads in rural areas, where many local suppliers are based, are often in poor condition, leading to delays in the delivery of goods and increased costs for businesses. Meanwhile, the country's energy infrastructure is notoriously unreliable, forcing many businesses to rely on expensive diesel generators to maintain operations. Through PPPs, the government can partner with private investors to fund critical infrastructure projects that directly support the needs of local suppliers.

For example, industrial parks or special economic zones (SEZs) could be developed through PPPs to provide local manufacturers with access to reliable power, water, and transportation networks. These zones could offer businesses the infrastructure they need to scale their operations efficiently while benefiting from reduced tariffs, tax incentives, and streamlined regulatory processes. Such partnerships could also facilitate the construction of storage and distribution centers, particularly for the agricultural sector, which suffers from high post-harvest losses due to inadequate cold storage facilities. By creating these zones and facilities, PPPs would enable local suppliers to compete more effectively in both domestic and international markets.

Additionally, PPPs can play a crucial role in addressing Nigeria's workforce development challenges. As local sourcing initiatives expand, the demand for skilled labor in industries such as manufacturing, logistics, and agriculture will continue to grow. However, many local suppliers lack access to workers with the technical and managerial skills required to operate efficiently. By partnering with educational institutions, vocational training centers, and private companies, the government can create programs that provide workers with the training they need to succeed in these industries.

One example of a successful PPP in workforce development is a partnership between a manufacturing company and a local technical college to design a curriculum tailored to the specific needs of the company's supply chain. This collaboration can equip students with practical skills such as machine operation, quality control, and production planning, ensuring that they are well-prepared to enter the workforce upon graduation. Apprenticeships and on-the-job training programs, supported by PPPs, can also help bridge the skills gap by allowing workers to gain hands-on experience while earning a wage. This dual approach benefits both businesses, which gain access to a skilled labor force, and workers, who receive valuable training and employment opportunities.

In addition to infrastructure and workforce development, PPPs can foster innovation within local supply chains. Innovation is essential for driving competitiveness and sustainability, particularly in industries like technology, agriculture, and manufacturing. Through PPPs, businesses can collaborate with research institutions, universities, and government agencies to develop new technologies, production methods, and processes that improve the efficiency and sustainability of supply chains. For instance, a PPP could fund research into precision agriculture techniques or new manufacturing technologies that reduce waste and energy consumption.

Another advantage of PPPs is their ability to share the risks and rewards of investments. Many private companies are hesitant to invest in local sourcing initiatives due to the perceived risks, such as market volatility, regulatory uncertainty, or the potential for supply chain disruptions. Through PPPs, the government can provide financial guarantees, subsidies, or tax incentives that mitigate these risks and encourage private investment. For example, the government could offer a guarantee to cover potential losses for private investors who finance infrastructure projects in rural areas. This risk-sharing arrangement makes local sourcing initiatives more attractive to private investors, helping to stimulate investment in critical sectors.

PPPs also offer opportunities for improving governance and accountability in local sourcing initiatives. By establishing clear roles and responsibilities for both public and private partners, PPPs can ensure that projects are managed efficiently and transparently. Governments can set the regulatory frameworks and policy guidelines that support the growth of local supply chains, while private companies bring their expertise, resources, and operational efficiencies to the table. Regular reporting and performance evaluations can help keep projects on track, ensuring that both parties meet their commitments and that the intended benefits are realized.

One notable example of a successful PPP in Nigeria is the Lagos Free Trade Zone (LFTZ). This public-private collaboration has attracted significant foreign investment and created thousands of jobs in industries such as manufacturing, logistics, and services. The LFTZ provides businesses with access to world-class infrastructure, streamlined regulatory processes, and proximity to major markets, demonstrating how PPPs can drive economic growth and support local sourcing initiatives. Another example is the Nigerian Incentive-Based Risk Sharing System for Agricultural Lending (NIRSAL), which was established to improve access to finance for farmers and agribusinesses. NIRSAL's partnership with commercial banks provides credit guarantees that reduce the risk of lending to the agricultural sector, enabling farmers to invest in new technologies and expand their production.

The success of these examples highlights the potential of PPPs to transform Nigeria's local supply chains. However, the effectiveness of PPPs depends on the broader policy and regulatory environment. Governments must create an enabling environment that fosters collaboration and reduces bureaucratic hurdles. This includes ensuring that contracts are fair and enforceable, regulatory processes are transparent and streamlined, and private investors have confidence in the long-term stability of government policies.

In conclusion, public-private partnerships are a powerful tool for promoting local sourcing and strengthening Nigeria's supply chains. By leveraging the expertise and resources of both the public and private sectors, PPPs can help address infrastructural, financial, and workforce development challenges, creating new opportunities for growth and development. As Nigeria continues to pursue its industrialization and economic diversification goals, PPPs will play an increasingly important role in shaping the future of the country's supply chains. Through collaboration, innovation, and shared risk, PPPs can help build stronger, more resilient supply chains that benefit businesses, workers, and communities across Nigeria.

CHAPTER 14

TRAINING AND WORKFORCE DEVELOPMENT: EQUIPPING NIGERIANS FOR SUPPLY CHAIN MANAGEMENT

As local sourcing becomes an integral part of Nigeria's economy, the need for a skilled workforce to manage supply chains effectively becomes increasingly important. For local suppliers to meet the growing demands of industries such as manufacturing, agriculture, and technology, they require a workforce that is not only technically proficient but also well-versed in supply chain management, logistics, and production planning. Training and workforce development are essential components for the success of local sourcing initiatives, as they ensure that the labor market can support the needs of modern, competitive industries.

One of the biggest challenges facing local suppliers in Nigeria is the skills gap. Many workers, particularly those in rural areas or in informal sectors, lack access to formal education and training programs that would equip them with the skills necessary to thrive in sectors like manufacturing, agriculture, and logistics. The absence of industry-specific training and vocational education limits the ability of these workers to contribute meaningfully to the economy and reduces the capacity of local suppliers to scale up their operations to meet demand. In addition, industries that require advanced technical skills, such as manufacturing and technology, often struggle to find workers with the specialized knowledge needed to operate modern machinery, manage production processes, or optimize supply chain operations.

To address this challenge, Nigeria must invest in vocational education and training (VET) programs that are specifically designed to meet the needs of local suppliers. Vocational training focuses on equipping workers with the practical skills and technical knowledge required to perform specific jobs, such as operating machinery, managing inventory, or ensuring quality control in production. These programs can be delivered through technical colleges, vocational schools, and industry-specific training centers, and they should be designed in collaboration with local businesses to ensure that the training aligns with industry needs.

Partnerships between businesses and educational institutions are critical for ensuring that VET programs provide relevant and up-to-date training. For example, a manufacturing company could collaborate with a local vocational school to design a curriculum that teaches students the skills required to operate the machinery used in the company's production processes. By aligning training programs with industry requirements, businesses can ensure that graduates are prepared to enter the workforce with the necessary skills to succeed. This type of collaboration not only benefits the business by providing a pipeline of skilled workers but also provides local workers with valuable opportunities for employment and career advancement.

Apprenticeships and on-the-job training programs are another effective method for developing the skills needed to support local sourcing initiatives. Apprenticeships allow workers to gain hands-on experience while earning a wage, making them an attractive option for both workers and employers. For businesses, apprenticeship programs offer an opportunity to train workers in the specific skills required for their operations, ensuring that employees are well-prepared to meet the demands of the job. In return, workers benefit from practical, real-world experience that enhances their employability and prepares them for long-term careers in supply chain management, manufacturing, and other sectors critical to Nigeria's economic development.

In addition to vocational training and apprenticeships, continuous professional development is essential for ensuring that the Nigerian workforce can keep pace with technological advancements and changing industry needs. As industries evolve and new technologies are introduced, workers must update their skills and knowledge to remain competitive. For example, in industries such as agriculture and manufacturing, new technologies like precision agriculture, automated machinery, and digital supply chain management tools are transforming how businesses operate. Workers who are trained in these new technologies will be better equipped to improve productivity, reduce waste, and contribute to the overall efficiency of supply chains.

Businesses can support ongoing professional development by offering training workshops, certification programs, and opportunities for workers to attend industry conferences or seminars. These programs not only help workers develop new skills but also enhance their understanding of industry's best practices and emerging trends. For example, a company might offer a training workshop on supply chain management software, teaching workers how to use digital tools to track inventory, manage logistics, and optimize procurement processes. By investing in continuous learning, businesses can ensure that their workforce remains adaptable and capable of responding to the ever-changing demands of the market.

Soft skills, such as communication, problem-solving, and teamwork, are also critical for the success of local sourcing initiatives. In supply chain management, effective communication is essential for coordinating activities between suppliers, manufacturers, distributors, and retailers. Workers who can communicate clearly and work well in teams are better equipped to manage the complexities of modern supply chains, where collaboration and coordination are key. Additionally, workers with strong problem-solving skills can help businesses identify and address bottlenecks, inefficiencies, or disruptions in the supply chain, ultimately improving the overall performance of the business.

Beyond formal education and training programs, governments and businesses must also focus on creating a culture of innovation and entrepreneurship. Many of Nigeria's local suppliers are small businesses or family-owned enterprises that have the potential to grow into larger, more competitive companies. By fostering a culture of entrepreneurship, governments and businesses can encourage local suppliers to adopt innovative business models, explore new markets, and invest in new technologies that improve their competitiveness. This can be achieved through initiatives such as business incubators, mentorship programs, and access to financing for startups and small enterprises.

Government support for workforce development is also essential for the success of local sourcing initiatives. The Nigerian government can play a key role in funding vocational training programs, developing industry-specific curricula, and providing financial incentives for businesses that invest in training their workers. Additionally, the government can create partnerships with international organizations, educational institutions, and private companies to improve access to high-quality training programs and increase the availability of skilled labor across key sectors.

One example of government intervention in workforce development is the creation of public-private partnerships (PPPs) that bring together government agencies, private businesses, and educational institutions to address the skills gap. For instance, a PPP could involve the government providing funding for a vocational training center, while a private company supplies the technical equipment and industry expertise needed to develop a curriculum. By working together, public and private entities can ensure that training programs are well-funded, well-designed, and aligned with industry needs, ultimately helping to build a skilled and capable workforce.

Educational institutions, such as universities, technical colleges, and research institutions, also play a critical role in workforce development. These institutions can collaborate with businesses to develop curricula that reflect the latest industry trends and technologies, ensuring that students are prepared for the demands of the modern workforce. Additionally, educational institutions can serve as hubs of innovation, conducting research and development that supports the growth of local industries and supply chains. By fostering strong partnerships between academia and industry, Nigeria can create a more dynamic and responsive education system that prepares students for careers in supply chain management, manufacturing, agriculture, and other key sectors.

Ultimately, the success of local sourcing in Nigeria depends on the ability of the workforce to meet the needs of businesses and industries. By investing in training and workforce development, Nigeria can build a labor force that is equipped with the technical, operational, and managerial skills needed to thrive in the country's evolving economy. This investment will not only benefit businesses by improving productivity and competitiveness but also provide workers with greater opportunities for employment, career advancement, and economic mobility.

In conclusion, workforce development is essential for the success of local sourcing initiatives in Nigeria. By building a skilled labor force that can support the needs of key industries, Nigeria can unlock the full potential of its local supply chains, create jobs, and drive economic growth. With the right mix of vocational training, apprenticeships, professional development, and government support, Nigeria can ensure that its workforce is prepared to meet the challenges and opportunities of the future.

CHAPTER 15

THE FUTURE OF LOCAL SOURCING IN NIGERIA: TRENDS AND PROJECTIONS

The future of local sourcing in Nigeria is poised for significant growth, driven by several key trends that are reshaping the global and domestic economic landscape. As businesses increasingly recognize the benefits of local sourcing—such as reducing costs, improving supply chain resilience, and supporting economic development—Nigeria is well-positioned to capitalize on these opportunities. However, the success of local sourcing initiatives will depend on how effectively Nigeria addresses its current challenges, such as infrastructure deficits, access to financing, and workforce development. In this final chapter, we will explore the key trends that will shape the future of local sourcing in Nigeria and provide projections for how these trends will influence the country's supply chains.

One of the most significant trends shaping the future of local sourcing in Nigeria is the increasing adoption of digitalization and technology across industries. As businesses embrace digital tools such as blockchain, artificial intelligence (AI), and the Internet of Things (IoT), local sourcing will become more efficient, transparent, and responsive to market demands. For example, blockchain technology can be used to track the provenance of goods and materials, providing businesses with greater visibility into their supply chains and ensuring that locally sourced products meet quality, ethical, and sustainability standards. By leveraging digital technologies, Nigerian businesses can improve their procurement processes, optimize inventory management, and reduce supply chain disruptions.

Artificial intelligence and machine learning also hold great promise for improving the efficiency of local supply chains. These technologies can be used to predict demand, manage logistics, and identify potential bottlenecks before they occur. For instance, an AI-powered system could analyze data on consumer behavior, weather patterns, or transportation routes to optimize the delivery of locally sourced goods. By reducing inefficiencies and improving forecasting accuracy, AI can help businesses minimize waste, lower costs, and improve their overall competitiveness.

Another important trend that will shape the future of local sourcing in Nigeria is the growing emphasis on sustainability and environmental responsibility. As concerns about climate change and resource depletion continue to rise, consumers and businesses are increasingly demanding products that are produced in an environmentally sustainable manner. Local sourcing aligns with this shift toward sustainability by reducing transportation emissions, promoting the use of locally available resources, and encouraging sustainable production practices. In the agricultural sector, for example, local sourcing can promote more sustainable farming methods, such as organic farming, agroforestry, and water conservation, all of which help reduce the environmental impact of food production.

Sustainability will also drive innovation in renewable energy, circular economic practices, and sustainable manufacturing. As Nigeria continues to develop its local supply chains, there will be growing opportunities for businesses to invest in clean energy solutions, such as solar or wind power, to reduce their reliance on fossil fuels. Additionally, circular economy practices such as recycling, reusing, and repurposing materials can help businesses minimize waste and reduce their environmental footprint. For instance, local manufacturers could adopt recycling programs that use recycled plastics or metals to produce new products, creating a closed-loop supply chain that benefits both the economy and the environment.

The rise of regional trade agreements, particularly the African Continental Free Trade Area (AfCFTA), is another trend that will influence the future of local sourcing in Nigeria. AfCFTA is designed to promote intra-African trade by reducing tariffs, harmonizing trade regulations, and eliminating non-tariff barriers. For Nigerian businesses, this presents a significant opportunity to expand their market reach beyond domestic borders and participate in regional supply chains. As regional trade grows, local suppliers will have access to larger markets, creating new opportunities for export growth and economic diversification. By building stronger supply chains within the African continent, Nigeria can position itself as a key player in the region's manufacturing, agriculture, and technology sectors.

Urbanization and the growth of Nigeria's middle class are also key factors that will shape the future of local sourcing. As more Nigerians move to urban areas and incomes rise, there will be increased demand for locally produced goods, particularly in sectors such as food, consumer products, and technology. This growing consumer base presents a significant opportunity for local suppliers to scale their operations and meet the needs of an expanding market. Moreover, the rise of e-commerce and digital platforms will make it easier for local suppliers to reach consumers directly, by passing traditional distribution channels and reducing the costs associated with logistics and retail.

Government policies will continue to play a critical role in shaping the future of local sourcing in Nigeria. The Nigerian government's commitment to industrialization, economic diversification, and job creation will drive further investments in infrastructure, education, and workforce development. Policies that promote local content, import substitution, and support for SMEs will be essential for ensuring that local suppliers can compete effectively in both domestic and international markets. However, the success of these policies will depend on their implementation, as well as the government's ability to create a stable and predictable regulatory environment that encourages private investment.

In terms of projections, we expect that local sourcing will continue to grow in importance across a range of industries in Nigeria. In the agricultural sector, local sourcing will become increasingly integrated into formal supply chains, with more businesses working directly with smallholder farmers to source raw materials and improve productivity. In manufacturing, we expect to see continued investments in local production capabilities, particularly in industries such as textiles, automotive, and consumer goods. The technology sector will also play a pivotal role in driving local sourcing, with Nigerian companies developing innovative solutions to meet the needs of local markets and compete globally.

In conclusion, the future of local sourcing in Nigeria is full of potential, but it will be shaped by several key trends, including the adoption of digital technologies, the rise of sustainability, the growth of regional trade, and the expansion of urban consumer markets. By embracing these trends and investing in the development of local supply chains, Nigeria can unlock new opportunities for economic growth, job creation, and industrial development. The success of local sourcing initiatives will depend on the collaboration of businesses, governments, and communities, as well as the ability to adapt to the changing global and domestic economic landscape. With the right strategies in place, Nigeria can harness the power of local sourcing to build a more prosperous, resilient, and sustainable economy for the future.

www.ingramcontent.com/pod-product-compliance
Lightning Source LLC
LaVergne TN
LVHW061527070526
838199LV00009B/405